Carole French & Reg

Tips on
TIPPING

A global guide to gratuity etiquette

Bradt Travel Guides Ltd, UK
The Globe Pequot Press Inc, USA

The Bradt story

The first Bradt travel guide was written in 1974 by George and Hilary Bradt on a river barge floating down a tributary of the Amazon. In the 1980s and '90s the focus shifted away from hiking to broader-based guides covering new destinations – usually the first to be published about these places. In the 21st century Bradt continues to publish such ground-breaking guides, as well as others to established holiday destinations.

Bradt authors support responsible travel, and provide advice not only on minimum impact but also on how to give something back through local charities. In this way a true synergy is achieved between the traveller and local communities.

First edition published February 2011
Bradt Travel Guides Ltd, 23 High Street, Chalfont St Peter, Bucks SL9 9QE, England
www.bradtguides.com
Published in the USA by The Globe Pequot Press Inc, 246 Goose Lane,
PO Box 480, Guilford, Connecticut 06437-0480

Text copyright © 2011 Carole French; Project Manager Anna Moores

British Library Cataloguing in Publication Data
A catalogue record for this book is available from the British Library

ISBN-13: 978 1 84162 210 1

Front cover Design by Artinfusion & James Nunn; image: James Slater/Getty Images
Designed and typeset from the authors' disc by Artinfusion
Production managed by Jellyfish Print Solutions and manufactured in India

Authors

Carole French

Carole French is a bit of a restless soul, 'commuting' between homes in the United Kingdom and Cyprus. She likes to travel, both for pleasure and business, and can often be found exploring cities and hotspots around the world.

Carole has written guidebooks covering destinations ranging from Paris to Morocco. She is a member of many professional bodies, including the British Guild of Travel Writers, and is an experienced magazine editor, having been at the helm of more than a dozen titles during her career. It was in the 1980s that she edited a magazine called *Caravan & Camping* and met Reg Butler who was one of her main contributors. Having worked with Reg for many years, Carole feels it a privilege to continue and complete *Tips on Tipping*.

Reg Butler

The late Reg Butler had enjoyed a long and varied career in journalism and was working on *Tips on Tipping* at the time of his death. Reg had travelled extensively over the years. He had been a hitchhiking backpacker and then worked 12 seasons as a tour manager before becoming a freelance journalist covering east and west Europe, Africa and Asia. He worked on contract with a New York publisher of international monthly commodity magazines and spent 27 years on contract to *The Wall Street Journal* covering Turkey and its neighbouring countries. *Tips on Tipping* contains a few anecdotes from his travels, which Reg wrote when beginning work on this guide.

Acknowledgements

With thanks to the following Bradt authors and contacts for checking individual entries: Jane Anderson, Daniel Austin, Judith Baker, Mark Baker, Larissa Banting, Kathleen Becker, Bermuda Department of Tourism (www.gotobermuda.co.uk), Andy Bostock, Hilary Bradt, Philip Briggs, Paul Brummell, Tim Burford, Helen Calderón, David Carter, Tim Clancy, Jacquie Cozens, Paul Crask, Steven Crook, Jaroslava Čujková (Slovak Tourist Board), Diana Darke, Ethel Davies, Edward Denison, Marc Di Duca, Carole Edrich, Royston Ellis, Marie-Lais Emond, Andrew Evans, Thammy Evans, Linda Fallon, Julian Fitter, Duncan Forgan, Nicky Gardner (*hidden europe*), Gillian Gloyer, Glenna Gordon, Gill Harvey, Tricia Hayne, Margaret Hebblethwaite, Annelies Hickendorff, Jeremy Hoare, Neal Hoskins, Carol Howland, Aisling Irwin, Lucija Jager (Slovenian Tourist Board), Journey Latin America (Jenny Hyden & Laura Rendell-Dunn), Annie Kay, Shweta Ganesh Kumar, Piers Letcher, Mikey Leung, Maria Lord, James Lowen, Kannika Mac (Tourism Thailand), Russell Maddicks, Lyn Mair, Lucy Mallows, Dan Marin (Transylvanian Wolf), Stella Martin, Chris McIntyre, Gordon McLachlan, Daniel McLaughlin, Ian Middleton, Laurence Mitchell, Paul Murray, David Orkin, Adrian Phillips, John Pitt, James Proctor, Catherine Quinn, Nick Redmayne, Annalisa Rellie, James Rice, Alexandra Richards, Juliet Rix, Nigel Roberts, David Sayers, Tim Skelton, Hilary Smith, Dorothy Stannard, Mike Stead, Neil Taylor, Kate Thomas, Emma Thomson, Lisa Voormeij, Laszlo Wagner, Nigel Wallis, Pauline Wee (Singapore Tourism Board), Lizzie Williams, Samantha Wilson, Sarah Woods and Kim Chan Young.

I would also like to thank the following Bradt authors for providing information on certain destinations: Ethel Davies (Libya), Mohamed El Hebeishy (Sudan), Sarah Irving (Palestine), Kirk Smock (Guyana), Tamara Thiessen (Borneo) and Mike Unwin (Swaziland).

Stuff your rucksack

🖱 www.stuffyourrucksack.com is a website set up by TV's Kate Humble which enables travellers to give direct help to small charities, schools or other organisations in the country they are visiting. Maybe a local school needs books, a map or pencils, or an orphanage needs children's clothes or toys – all things that can easily be 'stuffed in a rucksack' before departure. The charities get exactly what they need and travellers have the chance to meet local people and see how and where their gifts will be used.

The website describes organisations that need your help and lists the items they most need. Find out what they're looking for, contact the organisation to say you're coming and bring not only the much-needed goods but an extra dimension to your travels and the knowledge that in a small way you have made a difference.

Feedback request

This book is the most comprehensive guide to tipping available. It is continually being updated, and more and more countries being added. If there's a country you would like to see featured or you spot anything in the guide that has become out of date since it was published, contact author Carole French on ✉ carole@tipping-thebradtguide.com.

See also 🖱 updates.bradtguides.com and 🖱 www.tipping-thebradtguide.com.

Contents

Introduction

The practice of tipping can be a minefield. Who should you tip, and when? And when shouldn't you tip? When is a service charge included in your bill, and when not? And should you offer a bit extra even if a charge is included? How can travellers avoid causing embarrassment, offence or even accusations of bribery by offering a gratuity to the wrong person?

Some nationalities regard tipping as the norm, the most famous of which are perhaps American travellers, hotly followed by Canadians. In France there is a distinction between service and tipping, the latter being the *pourboire*. However, in some cultures tipping is considered offensive, unethical and even exploitative. Many hotels and restaurants, and even countries, have an official policy whereby service personnel are paid an acceptable wage and do not need to rely on tips to boost their income. Tipping is often banned. In Japan and Australia the offering of a tip is thought of as being a personal insult.

The trend in some cultures is changing, such as those in the Baltic states and other parts of Europe and Asia where, traditionally, tipping hasn't been a way of life. As more and more travellers visit these countries bringing with them personal customs, and local residents travel more themselves, then so tipping is becoming more acceptable. Of course, a gratuity should always be a reward for good service – for example, if someone has been particularly attentive, resolves a problem without hesitation or has helped to make your experience that extra bit special. But if you tip, where do you start when it comes to identifying what is right and what isn't?

How to use this book

Tips on Tipping gives an insight into tipping cultures in countries around the world, as well as including a dedicated chapter on cruising. Designed for both leisure and business travellers who want to avoid the pitfalls of tipping, it is the most comprehensive guide on the subject available. The guide includes a summary of different countries' cultures both for first-time visitors and for those who may not have visited a specific destination for a long time, as tipping customs in individual countries can change. It also covers the subject of gifts – when is a gift appropriate and when could it be considered a bribe? – and a few tips and personal anecdotes drawn from the late Reg Butler's and my own careers in travel.

While there are no hard-and-fast rules to tipping, and much depends on the location and one's personal experience at the time, a few pointers will be an invaluable aid when travelling the world. We hope you enjoy *Tips on Tipping* as much as we have enjoyed writing it for you.

A note about hotels: In this guide we have included recommended amounts to tip chambermaids and porters in the information panels at the start of each entry. In addition to this we have stated whether hotel bills are likely to be inclusive of service charges and/or whether an additional tip is expected.

For up-to-date **exchange rates** consult www.xe.com.

x

Africa

It is customary to tip in almost all African countries, although some automatically add a service charge and no further gratuity is expected, such as in Zambia. Some hotels actively ban tipping, so be sure to check. Most African countries work on around 10%, such as Mali, Algeria and Ghana, where tipping is known as *dash*. A few exceptions like South Africa look to nearer 15%, while in others, like Mozambique, it is not customary to tip at all. If you do tip, always do so in local currency (unless otherwise stated) as foreign money can be hard to exchange.

Algeria

🐚	**Currency**	Algerian dinar (DA), DZD; 1DA =100 santeem
🛏️	**Hotels**	Porter 90DA; Chambermaid 90DA
🍴	**Restaurants**	10%
🚗	**Taxis**	Round up

Offering a gratuity for good service in a **hotel** or **restaurant** environment is considered part of the culture, and because of this you should find that your meal will be brought to you with good grace and a smile. Expect to add 10% to your bill or round up to a similar amount. Also consider offering something to tour **guides** who will expect the standard 10% of the guide price, hotel room staff to whom you could leave upwards of 90DA, and in cafés. For **taxis**, you will need to make arrangements with drivers direct. It is a good idea to agree a price up front, in which case it is not necessary to tip, although if you do it is always appreciated. In the case of all gratuities it is best to hand it to the person for whom you intended it.

Algeria is steeped in traditions and customs. A warm and welcoming people, Algerians are likely to invite you to tea at their home if you become friendly. Be sure to remove your shoes when entering a private dwelling and take a small gift for the hostess. Chocolates, fruit or pastries are ideal, which you should give with your right hand. If you are offered food, eat with your right hand. In a business situation, men will often exchange prolonged handshakes followed by social conversation, before discussing business. Algerian women do not shake hands, especially with a male. If you are a woman attending a meeting you will find that your Algerian hosts will not shake your hand as a gesture of respect. Give and receive business cards with your right hand.

Angola

🚢	**Currency**	Angolan kwanza, AOA; 1AOA = 100 lwei
🏨	**Hotels**	Porter 200AOA; Chambermaid 200AOA
🍴	**Restaurants**	10%
🚗	**Taxis**	Round up

Angola is one of the world's poorest countries, which is reflected in the low wages earned by its often hard-working service personnel. Tipping, despite these salary levels, is not officially recognised or encouraged, but should you wish to offer a gratuity it would not cause offence and will always be accepted with gratitude, especially if you are able to tip in US dollars. Try to tip the member of staff in person – that way the tip is more likely to get into his/her pocket. A maximum of 10% of the bill in the case of **hotels**, **restaurants**, **taxi** and other similar services is appropriate. Hotel porters at the biggest hotels will hope for around US$2 to carry your bags. In the case of taxis, visitors need to make ad-hoc arrangements with drivers direct. As the fee should be decided up front, and would include a tip, no further gratuity is required, although if you do decide to offer a little extra it is always appreciated. Securing the services of a **tour guide** in Angola is rare, but if you do they do not generally expect to receive a tip.

In terms of gifts, while it is not considered a part of Angolan etiquette to give a gift it will always be appreciated, but this is best kept to personal situations only. A gift for the children of the household would be an ideal present. Business gifts are not expected; simply greet with a handshake, offer your business card and make social conversation before the commencement of a meeting. Meetings are generally held in the host company's business premises.

Benin

💰	**Currency**	CFA franc (Communauté Financière Africaine, CFA), XOF; CFA1 = 100 centimes
🛏	**Hotels**	Porter CFA600; Chambermaid CFA600
🍴	**Restaurants**	10%
🚗	**Taxis**	10%

Benin is a large country with stable economic growth, but it is underdeveloped and wages tend to be poor compared to Western standards. While tipping is considered a part of the country's culture, not all **hotels** and **restaurants** add a service charge. If they do there is no real reason to add anything further unless you wish to tip a particular individual. If no charge is included then opt for the industry standard of 10% of the bill, which you can do by rounding up or adding as an extra. For porters allow around CFA600 for helping with your luggage, and a similar amount for chambermaids per day. Give this directly to the individual. If taking a **taxi**, the easiest way to show your appreciation if the driver has been careful and helpful is to round up the fee to around 10% of the total. **Museum guides** will expect a tip; CFA1,000–2,000 is the norm.

Greetings are important and you are expected to say a general hello to everyone on entering a shop or business. Handshakes should always be offered on meeting and leaving people, whether male or female. For business meetings or eating at someone's home, dress should be formal. There will rarely be cutlery and you should use your right hand to take food from the communal bowl. If you are invited to take a drink outside someone's house it is common practice to pour a drop of the liquid onto the ground to ensure the spirits of the ancestors have something to drink.

Botswana

🐚	**Currency**	Botswana pula (P), BWP; P1 = 100 thebe
🏨	**Hotels**	Porter P5; Chambermaid P5–8
🍴	**Restaurants**	Service charge included, otherwise 10%
🚗	**Taxis**	Round up

In general, locals used to feel uncomfortable with the custom, but, as more and more travellers visit the country, so the tradition has become more acceptable. In **restaurants**, expect to tip around 10% over and above the bill, or a little more if you feel the service warrants it. Some restaurants have begun adding a service charge, so check before deciding what, if anything, to leave. **Hotels in the towns** work on about the same percentage. Hotel porters expect around P5 for helping with your luggage, while chambermaids usually receive about the same, or more, perhaps as much as P8.

Any trip to Botswana should include a safari tour. Your **tour guide** and **tracker**, and any **game rangers** you may come into contact with and who look after you, will appreciate a tip. Some, especially at the budget end of the market, may even rely on tips to boost a low level of income. Allow around P25 to P50 per day for each. In more upmarket lodges, allow up to P70 per guest per day if the service has been excellent. This is a guide only, and tips are never obligatory. Only tip if you feel the service has been good, and then do so only at the end of the trip. It is important that you don't tip after every game drive or activity – and equally vital that

Top tip

Check to see if tips go into a camp gratuity box to be divided amongst all the staff. If so, that may reflect on what you give.

5

you do check with the camp management about how tips are dealt with. Each camp or lodge will have a clear policy on tipping: some will have a tip box for all staff, others will ask you to tip the guides separately, and tip the general staff via a general box.

The art of greeting people is important in Botswana. When you first talk to someone, instead of rushing into whatever it is that you want to know, you should greet them leisurely, by bidding them good morning or afternoon, and enquiring after their wellbeing. If you are specially introduced to someone, you should use the three-part handshake common in southern Africa (see *Namibia*, page 28).

Should you be invited to dine with a family, it is best to use your discretion as to whether to bring a gift, or whether to reciprocate their generosity in some other way, such as by repaying them in kind or sending them a gift from your home country once you return.

Cameroon

🪙	**Currency**	Central African CFA franc (Communauté Financière Africaine, CFA), XAF; CFA1 = 100 centimes
🛎	**Hotels**	Porter CFA1,000–2,000; Chambermaid no tip
🍴	**Restaurants**	10%
🚗	**Taxis**	No tip

Hospitable and respectful, the people of Cameroon only tend to expect a gratuity if they have provided you with a memorable experience, and of course they will do their utmost to do just that whether you tip or not. The standard 10% of the total is acceptable if the service you receive in a hotel or restaurant, or on an organised tour, is especially good, although it is always considered discretionary. In some **hotels** and **restaurants** a service charge may be included, although it is not the norm. Always check before deciding how much, if anything, you feel you would like to leave. In Yaoundé, the capital, which sees more visitors than many other parts of the country, the practice of tipping is becoming more widespread. For porters you might like to leave CFA1,000–2,000, but at the present time neither chambermaids nor **taxi drivers** tend to expect a tip.

Cameroonians are a social people and will greet each other with much handshaking and conversation enquiring on the health of each other's families. If invited to a Cameroonian's home ideal gifts include an item from your own country, but do not offer wine or spirits unless you know the religion of your host and whether this would be acceptable to them. Offer your gift with the right hand. In a business situation, expect formality and be sure to offer a business card with your right hand.

Cape Verde

Currency	Cape Verdean escudo (CVE or $ after the numeral), CVE; 1CVE = 100 centavos	
▥ **Hotels**	Porter 100CVE; Chambermaid 100CVE	
⦙⦙ **Restaurants**	Service charge included or 10%	
⛟ **Taxis**	10%	

You will find that most people, such as waiters or taxi drivers, do not expect to receive anything extra and in fact may even try to give it back to you. However, if you feel the service has been particularly good offering a little money as a gratuity will probably be appreciated. Many **hotels** and **restaurants** will include a service charge in their bill, although you can leave extra for individuals at your discretion. If no charge is included then you can simply round up or leave about an extra 10% of the bill if you wish. It is entirely up to you. Porters and chambermaids are not generally tipped, but if you wanted to leave something consider around 100CVE per bag for porters or per day of your stay for chambermaids. **Tour guides and taxi drivers** are usually helpful, with the latter happy to assist you in carrying your luggage. A gratuity is a nice touch by way of a thank you. A good guide is to add 10% to the cost of your tour or taxi fare.

In social situations, men shake hands with men and the handshaking goes on for a long time, perhaps even for as long as the conversation. Two women, or a man and a woman, will generally shake hands as well as kissing on both cheeks, even if it is a first meeting. It is important to enquire after the other person's wellbeing.

Egypt

💰 **Currency**	Egyptian pound (E£), EGP; E£1 = 100 piastres
🏨 **Hotels**	Porter E£10; Chambermaid E£10
🍴 **Restaurants**	Service charge included, otherwise 10%
🚗 **Taxis**	Round up

Egypt is very much a *baksheesh* ('tip' or 'present') country and it is customary for every kind of service, however small. Salaries are low so *baksheesh* is the normal way of earning enough to live on. To the Western visitor, the constant whisper of '*baksheesh, baksheesh*' becomes an irritation. In fact, on a first visit it can come as a bit of a shock, but don't let it worry you. It's a way of life in Egypt, so try to be tolerant. It's a good idea to keep a few Egyptian pounds solely for the purpose in a spare pocket or easily accessible in a handbag, as

The baksheesh experience

During my first visit, my husband and I were dropped off by our private tour guide close to the Giza Pyramids so that we could hop on a couple of camels. We set off and immediately the camel drivers began yelling '*baksheesh, baksheesh*'. The camels seemed to get faster and faster. We jokingly guessed that, to the camel, the word '*baksheesh*' meant 'hurry'. We promised *baksheesh*, of course, the driver calmed, as did the camels, and we continued our exhilarating journey around the pyramids and to the Sphinx in a more leisurely fashion.

Carole French

9

that avoids having to open a wallet to show larger bills. The Egyptian pound splits into 100 piastres, with 25 and 50 piastre banknotes. It is these that are mostly used for baksheesh.

For **restaurants**, even if the bill already has an included 12% service charge, an additional 5% is normal. If a service charge is not levied, a waiter is usually tipped 10%, and room service waiters likewise. For **taxis**, the meter theoretically includes service, but just gracefully round up because the driver will rarely admit to having any small change and the extra Egyptian pound or two doesn't really hurt. The **tour guide** who has done a good job deserves a tip and it should be gauged on whether you have taken a half or whole day's excursion: 10% of the tour cost is a good guide. In luxury hotels, the baggage porter would expect around E£10.

At most **museums** and **archaeological sites**, attendants hold out their hand, discreetly and hope. If they have done nothing but stand there, ignore the outstretched hand. But often they perform some small service like pointing out a showcase, switching on a light or leading you into a temple side-chapel; E£5 would be a sufficient offering. Official **licensed guides** adhere to a fixed tariff set by the local tourist office. If you are planning to hire a guide's service then it is

On a Nile cruise, your guide will normally pay all on temple and tomb visits throughout the trip. The boat crew are tipped collectively at the end of the cruise so that all staff get a fair share. This is usually done by sealing your individual contribution in an envelope left with reception. Suggestions are around E£30–45 per person per day. A similar amount, or its equivalent, for your Egyptologist guide should be handed to him or her personally.

Top tip

Porters' relay

At a famous old hotel in Aswan, I was once housed in the modern annexe. When it was time to check out, a porter brought down my baggage to the annexe entrance but needed his tip there because that was the limit of his porterage zone. I suitably obliged. The porter relay then took me to the main hotel entrance, for which the second porter expected *baksheesh*. There I waited for the third porter who specialised in loading bags into taxis and also expected *baksheesh*. Again I obliged. But Egypt is worth it.

Reg Butler

good practice to consult the tourist office for the most current fee to pay; the tarrif does not include a tip. Tour operators will use the same guides. Many are excellent linguists and often have spent several university years in ancient Egyptian studies. They can bring every feature of temples and tombs to fascinating life. In short, they are worthy of a tip – reckon on around 10% of the cost of the tour. However, in all tourist locations you'll be accosted by charming youths or schoolkids who want to practise English, and offer to show you around. These would-be guides usually expect *baksheesh*, even if they offer their services as a friendly gesture. It is arguable as to whether you should encourage this, but if you wish to accept their 'service' then around E£5–10 would be appropriate. It is best to hire an official guide.

If you are invited into an Egyptian's home for dinner, a gift of good quality chocolates, sweets or pastries would be appropriate, but not flowers. It is considered a compliment if you have second helpings of food, but you should leave a small amount on your plate when you have finished, otherwise it will continue to be refilled! It is also worth noting that adding salt to your food is taken as an insult.

Eritrea

✆	**Currency**	Eritrean nakfa (Nfa), ERN; Nfa1 = 100 cents
🛏	**Hotels**	Porter Nfa5; Chambermaid Nfa5
🍴	**Restaurants**	10%
🚗	**Taxis**	Nfa5–10

The people of Eritrea are accustomed to the practice of tipping, although it is more prevalent in the larger cities and less common in rural communities. The larger or more expensive **hotels** and **restaurants** that are used to welcoming tourists are more inclined to add a service charge of 10% to the bill before it is presented to you. You may choose to leave extra to an individual who has given you above average service; a hotel porter for example, or a chambermaid who has kept your room clean and tidy for you during your stay. Around Nfa5 per bag for a porter and Nfa5 per day for a chambermaid should do the trick and will almost certainly be appreciated as many service personnel earn very little and tips help their lifestyle enormously. If you do tip extra it is wise to give it direct. Where a service charge is not included in the bill add 10% of the total which, on average, will equate to about Nfa15–20. For **taxis**, you can offer a Nfa5 or Nfa10 tip if you have specifically contracted a driver to take you on your journey. If, however, you take one of Eritrea's urban taxis which always follow a predetermined route for a fixed fare, there is no need to tip.

Eritreans are warm and hospitable and people will often invite you into their homes to drink coffee or share food. A gift for the hosts of cakes, coffee or other foods would be appreciated, as would pens or sweets for the children.

Ethiopia

🛥	**Currency**	Ethiopian birr, ETB; birr 1 = 100 cents
🏨	**Hotels**	Porter birr 2; Chambermaid birr 2
🍴	**Restaurants**	Service charge included, otherwise 10%
🚗	**Taxis**	Round up

Tipping is entirely discretionary, but always appreciated. Take care not to offend though – Ethiopians are friendly and like to assist you if they can. That said, in tourist areas where many Ethiopians have become accustomed to receiving tips for the smallest of favours, they may be disgruntled if you don't oblige. In tourist **hotels** run by the government and finer dining **restaurants** there is usually a service charge added to prices and no obligation to tip more. If you do tip, the usual yardstick of 10% is actually generous, but you may feel it is appropriate. Try to give it directly to the waiter or waitress – birr 2 is about right. In **cafés** leave small change on the table.

If you visit **historical sites** with an organised group you will probably find the guides, who are all qualified and highly knowledgeable, will be working to a standard tipping rate of at least birr 100 a day. Expect to tip a **private guide** at least birr 20 for the first couple of hours, which should increase by about birr 10 for every hour you are with him after that. Agree a rate in advance to avoid any pressure to tip more at the end, which can and does happen.

It is usual to greet people with a handshake, although between opposite sexes the man should wait to see whether the woman extends her hand. Don't launch straight into an enquiry; it is polite to ask after the other person's health and family first. If you stay with a family, respond to their generosity in kind. You could take them out for a meal or ask them if there is anything that they'd like from your country, and remember to send it when you get home.

13

The Gambia

Africa | THE GAMBIA

🖳 **Currency**	Gambian dalasi (D), GMD; D1 = 100 bututs
🛏 **Hotels**	Porter D10; Chambermaid D10
🍴 **Restaurants**	Service charge included, otherwise 5–10%
🚗 **Taxis**	Round up

The Gambia has a fairly defined tipping culture, where most services performed well are rewarded with a *cadeau*, a small tip or gift. In **hotels** and the more expensive **restaurants** a 10% service charge is usually included in the bill you receive, and if you wish to tip further it is left entirely to your discretion. Allow about D1 or 5–10% of the total bill in local currency. A guide for tipping other service personnel is D10 for a porter per bag, and D10 per day for your chambermaid.

When out and about, it's a good idea to hire an official hotel tourist guide as this ensures you are not bothered by unofficial would-be guides who may not have the knowledge but will expect a tip nonetheless. There are a lot of them about and at first they may appear to be just friendly, but their motive is, by and large, financial. Only tip if you have received a service that warrants it. An **official guide** should be given a tip of about 5–10% of his fee, although this should be given only if the service was very good, and if you hire one with specialist knowledge then you might feel it is more appropriate to add anything up to 20%.

Greetings are important in Gambian society, so if you don't speak the language, just say hello and shake hands (right hands only) with a smile. If you are invited into someone's home, use only your right hand for eating from the communal pot. If you visit a village, speak with the village elder first of all, taking him a small gift, such as kola nuts, which are readily available for sale.

Ghana

&#9880;	**Currency**	Ghanaian cedi (C), GHS; C1 = 100 pesewas
&#127976;	**Hotels**	Porter C2; Chambermaid C2
&#127860;	**Restaurants**	Service charge included or 5–10%
&#128664;	**Taxis**	5–10%

Ghanaians are a friendly and helpful people, but are not well paid. Even taking into consideration the fact that wages are relative to the local cost of living, the sums are small. When visiting Ghana, therefore, you may like to consider offering a gratuity to someone who has earned it through looking after your needs. Many **hotels** and **restaurants** which cater for tourists will automatically add a 5% to 10% service charge to the bill, which should go to the hotel staff waiter, but you may like to use your discretion to tip further if you feel it is right. You may take a **taxi** or join a tour during your stay, and if the service provided by the driver or **guide** was good then around 10% of the total price would not go amiss.

Ghanaians have a variety of ways to greet friends and colleagues, but with foreign visitors they will almost always offer a handshake. Depending on their religion, some men may not shake hands with a female visitor. Gifts, both when dining with a Ghanaian family in their home or in a business environment, are not expected, but if you are visiting a private home and wish to make a small offering then confectionery for your host's children is ideal. Gifts and business cards are presented with the right hand.

Kenya

🏦 **Currency**	Kenya shilling (KSh), KES; KSh1 = 100 cents
🏨 **Hotels**	Porter KSh50; Chambermaid KSh50
🍴 **Restaurants**	10%
🚕 **Taxis**	10%

On arrival, if you are met at the airport by a pre-arranged transfer driver, be prepared to give a gratuity of around KSh100. If you plan to make your transfer by **taxi**, bargain for the best price, and having agreed the fee there's no need to tip further. Tipping in Kenyan shillings rather than a foreign currency always helps to smooth the way. Do not tip in foreign coins, which may be difficult for recipients to change.

Mainstream **hotels** and **restaurants** usually include at least a 10% service charge when calculating the bill. For exceptional service that is friendly and attentive, 50 shillings or so extra is appropriate, but at your discretion. If service is not included, restaurant waiters in tourist and business establishments are accustomed to receiving a 10% tip. For bar staff, give around KSh20–30 per round of drinks. About KSh50 or so is usual for porters, and likewise for room staff. If going on safari, most **camps** and **lodges** will include a service charge in your accommodation rate, leaving you to tip around KSh100 for waiting staff. Camps and lodges often have staff tip boxes – check how much to leave, as there's no general standard. A collection is normally made for the **guide driver** on a one-day excursion. His usual gratuity is around KSh150 per person for the day. Of course, not all visitors to Kenya will be on an organised package safari. Independent travellers on private tours will not normally need to tip in places such as restaurants and bars. On a **climbing trek**, it could cost each member of the party the

Top tip

The basic schooling of some village children in Kenya is hampered by the lack of ballpoint pens, pencils and small notebooks. For those wishing to help, see page v.

equivalent of US$18 per day to tip the full climbing crew (consisting of leading guide and his assistant, porters and a cook). This collective tip is presented at the end of the trip. During an **offshore fishing trip**, the crew will cheerfully prepare and put on ice any fish you catch and want to eat back at the hotel. Tipping of the crew is accepted with thanks but is not obligatory.

If you are invited to a business associate's home do not bring flowers as they are normally used to express condolences.

Exchanging greetings is extremely important in Kenyan culture; you should ask someone how they are and possibly exchange small talk before getting to the point. If you are invited to dinner at an expat's house, bring the kind of gift that you would at home. Elsewhere, it is best to use your instincts when reciprocating your host's generosity – you could bring a gift, try to repay them in kind, or remember to send them something from your own country when you return home.

Liberia

🕮	**Currency**	Liberian dollar (LD), LRD; 1LD = 100 cents
▥	**Hotels**	Porter 50LD; Chambermaid 50LD
🍴	**Restaurants**	10%
🚗	**Taxis**	Round up

Liberia doesn't really have a tipping culture, but is beginning to with the arrival of returned Liberian refugees from the USA. It is generally expected that expats and visitors will tip in **restaurants** and for services received in **hotels**. Offer around 10% in restaurants; rounding up the bill is acceptable. Consider 50LD per bag for hotel porters and about the same per day for chambermaids. Note that in cities like Monrovia the US dollar is widely used, but in rural areas you should use only the Liberian dollar, known affectionately as 'the liberty'. If you're paying in US dollars, you should tip – ideally with smaller change in LD.

Tour **guides** should always be tipped; consider around 10% of the amount you paid for your tour, while for **taxis** it is best to round up the fare. In Monrovia you might encounter young men who 'help' you park and watch your car for you – you are under no obligation to pay them, but if you choose to give – in some cases it can avoid a troublesome situation – offer 20–100LD.

People greet one another with a Liberian handshake, which involves a snap of the index fingers. Government officials tend to stick to the Western handshake. Liberians are a hospitable people and if you become friendly with them they will often invite you to dine with them. Take a gift with you – fruit or a bag of rice, the latter being the staple Liberian food. If you have not brought a gift, offer to buy everyone soft drinks, which will be greeted with much appreciation. If invited to eat from a communal dish, use your right hand only.

Libya

🖎 **Currency**	Libyan dinar LYD; LYD1 = 1,000 dirhams	
🏨 **Hotels**	Porter 500 dirhams; Chambermaid 500 dirhams	
🍴 **Restaurants**	10%	
🚕 **Taxis**	No tip	

Libya, or, to give it its full name, the Great Socialist People's Libyan Arab Jamahiriya, is a country that is seeing an increase in tourism and where once tipping was far from encouraged it is gradually becoming more acceptable. Many of the larger **hotels** and their staff are now more used to welcoming overseas visitors to whom tipping is the norm. The same can be said for **restaurants**, especially in the capital Tripoli. Reckon on no more than 10% of the amount you are paying for the service; however, any more would be inappropriate. Libyans are a friendly people and will reward you with a beaming smile whatever the amount so tip what you feel the service warrants. In the main, **taxi drivers** do not expect a tip, neither do porters or chambermaids, but if you feel you would like to give a small amount then consider 10% of the taxi fare and around 500 dirhams per bag/day for them respectively. Tipping in more rural areas is not really expected.

In terms of giving gifts, your host or hostess is sure to appreciate confectionery, pastries or flowers, but alcohol is best avoided as it isn't officially allowed into the country. In a business situation you wouldn't be expected to shake hands, and certainly not with a female associate, but it is a good idea to have a supply of business cards.

Madagascar

🪙	**Currency**	Malagasy ariary (Ar), MGA; 1Ar = 5 iraimbilanja
🛎	**Hotels**	Porter 100–500Ar; Chambermaid 100Ar
🍴	**Restaurants**	Service charge included, otherwise 10%
🚕	**Taxis**	Round up

Service personnel have traditionally not expected tips, although this is changing as more and more travellers visit the island and bring with them customs from their own countries. Nowadays, a service charge of around 10–15% is added to bills in European-style **hotels** and **restaurants**, and although there is no necessity to tip further if you have received an exceptional service, you may like to round up or leave a little extra, say 50Ar, for the waiter or waitress. **Taxi drivers** in the main do not expect a tip and will provide you with a friendly service no matter what. If you feel you would like to offer something then the best advice would be to round up.

Baggage handlers, however, are a little more cunning. They have become wise to travellers who, having just landed, are not yet acquainted with the way the Malagasy do things, and have become adept at showing disappointment with a small tip. Remember the wages and the cost of living are much, much lower than in many other countries. The average Malagasy earns the equivalent of

Top tip

A trick much loved by porters at Tana airport is to suggest you tip them a euro, knowing that travellers are more likely to offer this 'small' amount than its apparent 'larger' amount in local currency.

around £3 or US$5 per week. It is, therefore, easy for the Western traveller to over-tip. Someone who carries your bag to your car at an airport, or your bag to your room in a hotel, should receive between 100 and 500Ar. When tipping **tour guides**, the equivalent of US$5 or so a day if they have provided a good service is about right, which although generous, rewards them for their knowledge and helpfulness. In rural Madagascar the locals still tend to refer to the old currency, the Malagasy Franc, which is worth about one-fifth of an Ariary.

The Malagasy greet with a handshake as in much of the world, but to be particularly polite a two-handed shake is used: shake hands as normal while gripping your right elbow or forearm with your left hand. It is also considered polite to give or receive items (including money) with both hands. Direct refusal of any offer is considered rude. If invited to dine or stay with a Malagasy family a gift of money in return for their hospitality is entirely acceptable.

Malawi

💰 **Currency**	Malawian kwacha (Mk), MWK; Mk1 = 100 tambala	
Hotels	Porter Mk30; Chambermaid Mk30	
Restaurants	10%	
Taxis	Round up	

Tipping has become an established custom in Malawi and you will find service personnel in **hotels**, **lodges** and **upmarket safari camps** will expect a little something for their efforts, although it is discretionary. Staff will never openly solicit a tip and the amount, should you wish to tip, is based entirely on the level of service you have received. The unwritten rule of 10% is usually about right. Care should be taken in the sum you choose. The kwacha has a very low exchange rate to many Western currencies, so check rates and be sure not to leave an amount that might appear derisory. Wages are low so a good tip goes a long way. Other people you might like to tip around Mk20–30 are **drivers**, petrol station attendants and anyone who allows you to take their photograph, but on no account offer anything to an official as this could very well land you in jail on corruption charges.

Gifts are often appropriate in a business environment, although not automatically expected, and do take a gift of something from your own country or a food basket to the host or hostess if invited to someone's home.

Mali

🪙 **Currency**	West African CFA franc (Communauté Financière Africaine, CFA), XOF; CFA1 = 100 centimes	
🛎 **Hotels**	Porter CFA500; Chambermaid CFA500	
🍴 **Restaurants**	10%	
🚗 **Taxis**	Round up	

Bargaining is a way of life for most services, and once a price has been agreed no further tip is necessary. Such is the case for **taxis**. However, people engaged in the service industry on a fixed wage may well look for tips to boost their income, so you might like to tip people who have given you a genuinely good service. It is customary to tip waiting staff around 10% of the bill in **hotels** and **restaurants**, which should equate to approximately CFA500. The practice of tipping is, however, entirely discretionary, but it is worth keeping in mind that the average wage is around US$3 per day for waiting staff. Around CFA500 is therefore a generous tip. You might like to offer CFA3,000–5,000 for a local **guide** per day; official guides are likely to expect more. CFA10,000 should be the maximum you pay. Also consider around CFA500 for a bellboy or **porter** for assisting with your bags.

The people of Mali are hospitable, but shows of gratitude can cause embarrassment. Try to pay for any hospitability you receive in kind. You could offer a gift of green tea and sugar if dining with a family. For longer stays of more than one night, consider buying staple food for the family, such as a sack of rice. If you would prefer to pay for your stay, around CFA3,000–5,000 per night given surreptitiously to the head of the household would be about right.

Mauritius

&#x1F4B8;	**Currency**	Mauritian rupee (Rs), MUR; Rs1 = 100 cents
&#x1F3E8;	**Hotels**	Porter Rs100; Chambermaid Rs50
&#x1F37D;	**Restaurants**	Service charge included, otherwise 5–10%
&#x1F695;	**Taxis**	Round up

You'll find Mauritians to be friendly and helpful, so a stay at your favourite hotel or a meal in a chosen restaurant is sure to be a pleasurable experience. Waiter service is usual in **restaurants**, and you should consider a tip of 5–10% if you wish to leave a gratuity. It is entirely discretionary, however, and you are under no obligation. Do check that a service charge is not included in the bill before you tip, as some establishments add this as a matter of course. Tipping is not expected in **cafés** or coffee shops. Many **hotels** prefer that you do not tip individual members of staff but rather that you place any tips in a tipping box at the hotel reception. It is best to check your hotel's policy.

You'll find that **taxi drivers** do not expect a tip, but if you wish to offer one then it will almost always prompt a wide smile and exclamations of gratitude. Rounding up the taxi fare is a good idea. It is customary, however, to tip **porters**. You may find hotel porters are less inclined to hover in the expectation of a tip, unlike airport porters. Allow about Rs100 depending on how many items of luggage they have carried for you.

In business, small gifts may be given on conclusion of a deal, but only give and receive with your right hand. Taking a gift for the host or hostess when dining privately is not customary.

Morocco

⌖	**Currency**	Moroccan dirham (MAD or م.د), MAD; MAD1 = 100 centimes
🏨	**Hotels**	Porter MAD10; Chambermaid MAD10–20
🍴	**Restaurants**	Service charge included, otherwise 10%
🚗	**Taxis**	Round up

Morocco's hotels and restaurants vary in standard enormously, as do the prices. Some are quaint and traditional, which if you love going off the beaten track and experiencing the country's rustic charm will be a delight for you, while others ooze international five-star luxury. Views on tipping are pretty much the same. In the larger **hotels** and **restaurants**, and especially those found in the larger cities like Marrakech and Casablanca, and popular holiday locations like Agadir, you'll almost certainly find a 10% service charge added to the bill. There's no need to leave more. If your waiter has been particularly attentive you might like to leave around MAD10–20, but avoid adding a sum to the bill or rounding up as it may not reach the person for whom you intended it. Better to leave some change in the local currency or give it direct.

Other personnel who you might like to tip are hairdressers and barbers, cloakroom attendants and porters, to each of whom you should offer a few dirhams. In the case of **taxi drivers**, it is customary, and much easier, to round up the bill. It is always appreciated.

In terms of business and social etiquette, most Moroccans follow Islam and this should, of course, be respected. Ramadan is an important event in the calendar, and you may find that your host will be observing a period of fasting when you meet. Business meetings are often accompanied by an invitation to dine, either before or after.

Charmers

Morocco is a wonderful place if you are looking for a photo opportunity, but when a local is involved, expect to tip. Be sure to ask permission too. The snake charmers of Casablanca or Marrakech are practised at posing for you. You can't help but smile at their antics quite clearly performed in the expectation of a tip. And remember if you don't tip you might just have one of those rather alarming snakes placed around your neck. It's worth a tip in my book.

Carole French

If you are invited to dine in a person's home, always dress smartly, arrive promptly, take a small gift of fruit, pastries or nuts – never alcohol unless you know that your host drinks – and be prepared to remove your shoes.

Mozambique

	Currency	Mozambican metical novo (Mtn), MZN; Mtn1 = 100 centavos
	Hotels	Porter Mtn25; Chambermaid Mtn25
	Restaurants	10%
	Taxis	10%

Mozambique is a popular tourist destination. Its hotel and restaurant staff and its taxi drivers are used to dealing with tourists, and are accustomed to the practice of tipping, but although it is a fairly standard way of showing appreciation to the country's service personnel, it is not obligatory. If you have received good service then tip, if not then do not feel under any pressure to do so. It is entirely discretionary. The rule of thumb is 10% in **hotels** and **restaurants**, while hotel bellboys and **porters** ought to receive around Mtn25 per item of luggage, and chambermaids about the same or a little more per day. Tour **guides** tend to receive more so reckon on about Mtn100–150 per day if you are happy with their service.

Mozambicans of the same age and gender shake hands enthusiastically during greetings. Elderly people are accorded a lot of respect, so when meeting people of older generations it is important to show deference by extending your hand and bowing. If visiting someone's home, use your knowledge of their social position to decide upon an appropriate gift or way of repaying their generosity.

Namibia

🪙	**Currency**	Namibia dollar (N$), NAD; N$1 = 100 cents
🛏️	**Hotels**	Porter N$10; Chambermaid N$20
🍽️	**Restaurants**	10%
🚗	**Taxis**	Small change

Tipping is expected only in upmarket tourist establishments. If a service charge is included in a bill, in a **hotel** or **restaurant** for example, an additional tip is not usually given. Otherwise, add 10% or so as a tip for restaurant waiters. Most visitors come for game viewing. A few tour **guides**, game rangers and trackers who work in more budget-orientated places may rely on tips for their income; for most, tips are a welcome bonus on top of their basic wage. If a guide gives a really good service, then reckon about N$100 per person per day. Tipping of staff in national parks and reserves is officially prohibited. Be aware that foreign currencies, with the exception of the South African rand, are not accepted at state-owned rest camps and they have no money-changing facilities. The Namibian dollar is fixed to and equals the South African rand. The Namibian dollar and the rand are the only legal tender and both can be used freely.

Greetings are very important when you first meet someone. You should open with 'Good morning/afternoon' and 'How are you?' before getting down to business. There is a gentle, three-part handshake: the two people take each other's right hand, as for a normal handshake, but just shake once, up and down. Then, leaving their thumbs linked, they change their grip until their arms make a right-angle. Each then grasps the other person's thumb and the top of their hand firmly. Finally, this is relaxed, with thumbs still interlinked, and the hands are dropped back into one last normal 'shake'.

Nigeria

🖉 **Currency**	Nigerian naira (₦), NGN; ₦1 = 100 kobo
🏨 **Hotels**	Porter ₦100 per bag; Chambermaid ₦100
🍴 **Restaurants**	Service charge included, otherwise 5–10%
🚕 **Taxis**	Round up

In the larger **hotels** and upmarket **restaurants** a service charge of 10% is almost always added to your bill, and you may find that even smaller establishments do the same. Any additional tip is discretionary. Of course, if someone has provided you with an exceptional service, such as a waiter in a hotel or restaurant, or a porter, it is probably in the expectation of a tip. Nigerians as a rule do not tip themselves, but you may wish to do so. Tipping 5–10% is about right. Offer around ₦100 or so to porters. For **taxi** journeys it is best to agree a price ahead of the journey, and be aware that tourists tend to be quoted a higher rate so you may feel a tip isn't really appropriate. The practice of tipping is often referred to as *dashing* in Nigeria, which is also the term given to a bribe. Bribery in Nigeria is an issue, but as a visitor you will probably not encounter a situation where you will be expected to offer a bribe. An exception of sorts, however, is that you might be expected to offer a tip ahead of a service provided by someone like a museum **guide**. The only other time you might find yourself wishing to offer money is to someone who allows you to take their photograph. Consider around US$5, equivalent to about ₦750.

Greetings are all-important and saying 'hello', asking 'how you are', and questions about your family are all customary at the beginning of a conversation. It's usual to take a gift to someone's home if going for a meal or to stay. Fruit, kola nuts or chocolates are ideal. Always present gifts with your right hand or both hands, never your left.

Rwanda

🐚 **Currency**	Rwandan franc (Rfr), RWF; Rfr1 = 100 centimes	
🗠 **Hotels**	Porter Rfr500–550; Chambermaid Rfr500–50	
🍴 **Restaurants**	10%	
🚗 **Taxis**	10%	

The industry standard of 10% in **hotels**, **restaurants** and to **taxi drivers** applies in Rwanda, a country that is attuned to the practice of leaving a gratuity to show an appreciation of service. It is, however, discretionary and accepted that if a customer doesn't tip, he or she probably has good reason not to. As a guide allow Rfr500–550, which is equivalent to around US$1, an accepted form of currency, for porters per item of luggage and for chambermaids. Trek and tour **guides** will expect anything between Rfr3,000 and Rfr5,000 per day.

Extended greetings during conversation are the norm and it is considered rude to ask for something in a shop, or to ask for directions, without first enquiring as to the person's health and wellbeing. If you are invited to dinner at someone's house, use your discretion as to whether you should bring a gift or try to repay your host in kind.

St Helena

✆	**Currency**	St Helena pound (£), SHP; £1 = 100 pence
⌕	**Hotels**	Porter £1; Chambermaid £1
⏍	**Restaurants**	10%
🚗	**Taxis**	Round up

British visitors to St Helena will find its currency easy to get to grips with because the St Helena pound is fixed at parity with the sterling pound. Dining in **hotels** or **restaurants** is all rather relaxed, with tipping and its amount being entirely discretionary, although 10% works well. **Taxi drivers** are usually proud of their island and happy to give you lots of snippets of information without any suggestion of a tip. If they help you with your luggage, however, you might like to round up the fare as a show of respect and gratitude.

If you befriend an islander and are invited to dinner, bring along a small gift – standards such as a bottle of wine or chocolates are fine.

São Tomé & Príncipe

🕿	**Currency**	Santomean dobra (written as $, after the amount), STD; 1$ = 100 centimos
🛏	**Hotels**	Porter 2,000$; Chambermaid 2,000$
🍴	**Restaurants**	10%
🚗	**Taxis**	Round up

Whilst a healthy tourism infrastructure is emerging, the practice of tipping, is not yet that developed and so you should use your discretion if you wish to reward someone. A tip for good service is unlikely to offend, but it can cause embarrassment. The best practice is to round up if the service has been good. That way it doesn't appear to be an obvious tip, but can still be taken as a gesture that indicates that you are pleased and satisfied with the service you have received. Waiters in some of the larger, more luxurious **hotels** where international practices tend to dominate are getting used to receiving tips, usually of around 10% of the bill.

Other service personnel you might like to tip include porters at around 2,000$, chambermaids at 2,000$, and hairdressers, who expect around 5,000$. As regards **taxis**, unless you are hiring a cab for a special journey, in which case you need only to round up, there is no need to tip.

Top tip

In general Santomeans are friendly and laidback, and really appreciate it if you manage to pick up a few local expressions. Giving the reply *léve-léve* (literally, 'slowly-slowly', meaning 'fine') to the question *Tudo bem?* is bound to go down well.

Seychelles

🐚 **Currency**		Seychellois rupee (SR), SCR; SR1 = 100 cents
🛏️ **Hotels**		Porter SR12; Chambermaid SR10
🍴 **Restaurants**		Service charge included
🚗 **Taxis**		Round up

In many respects, the Seychelles is an uncomplicated place to visit. Whether you are staying in a **hotel**, dining in a **restaurant**, enjoying a coffee or a cooling drink in one of its lovely outdoor **cafés** or taking a **cab** then you will find that a service charge is already included in the price you pay. The standard rate is between 5% and 10%. No further tipping is expected nor customary; however, should you wish to offer a small tip then this will not cause offence. If you plan to take a tour of the area, perhaps stopping off to see local handicrafts like the batik fabric or snail-shell jewellery for which the Seychelles is famous, you might like to hire a cab driver and his car for the day. The price quoted will include a service charge, although do check and then gauge whether you wish to round up or offer more if your driver has been especially attentive and helpful. If you take a tour you might like to tip the **guide**. Consider around 10% of the cost of the tour, but take into consideration the duration and number of people on the trip.

Conducting business in the Seychelles is usually fairly casual, although punctuality is important. The giving of gifts would not be expected. If you are invited to dine in someone's home, however, it is a good idea to bring a small gift as a token of your appreciation.

Sierra Leone

🪙	**Currency**	Sierra Leonean leone (Le), SLL; Le1 = 100 cents
🛏	**Hotels**	Porter Le5,000; Chambermaid Le5,000
🍽	**Restaurants**	10%
🚗	**Taxis**	Round up

Tipping is not standardised in Sierra Leone, and **hotels** and **restaurants**, including those in the capital Freetown, do not include a service charge. If you wish to tip then consider a maximum of 10% of the total bill if you have enjoyed the service. The latter, of course, is always discretionary. As regards **taxis** and **tours**, it is not expected that you will tip the driver or guide if sharing their expertise with others. However, if you hire their services privately and you have been served well then consider offering up to Le5,000.

If invited to someone's home for dinner consider it an honour and always take a gift of sugar, rice or soap for the host. If the event is a wedding then notes in an envelope should be given.

South Africa

🪙	**Currency**	South African rand (R), ZAR; R1 = 100 cents
🛎️	**Hotels**	Porter R5; Chambermaid R5
🍽️	**Restaurants**	10%
🚗	**Taxis**	Round up or 10%

South Africans, and in particular those who live in the cities and tourist spots, are usually worldly and as such the custom of tipping is widely known to them and established. In **restaurants** you will find that a 10% tip is expected, and usually warranted, while in **hotels** tipping staff is regarded as discretionary and left to guests to decide. Few hotels and restaurants apply a service charge, although it is becoming more widespread, especially if there are many people in your party. Check the bill before deciding on what to leave. It is, however, customary to tip a hotel porter a few rand for helping you with your luggage, and chambermaids if they have kept your room spotless during your stay. About R5–10 should do the job nicely, but be sure to give it to the person for whom you intend it.

There are many tours and safaris available in South Africa, and you will find it is customary to tip your **guide** between R30 and R50 per person per day, depending on the status of the establishment rather than the quality of the service. This is paid at the end of the tour. The

Top tip

Do not confuse a kombi taxi with a saloon taxi. Kombi taxis can be seen everywhere but actually act as buses travelling along set routes. No tip is necessary; just the payment of the fare.

same is said for **car guards**, identified by their official badge and dress. By offering a guard R2–5 they will watch over your car while you are away, the money given to them on your return. You may find a few opportunist types are quick to offer help with parking your car, especially in tourist spots, but be aware they are not official and you don't have to tip them unless you feel generous. A similar amount, R2–5, is generally given to **garage attendants** who wash your car windscreen and check your oil and water while filling up with fuel. **Taxi drivers** tend not to expect a tip, but then the fares are usually high. If you wish to tip, by far the easiest way is to round up the fare.

The giving of gifts is a pleasant custom amongst friends or acquaintances, especially if you are invited to someone's home to eat. Most people take a bottle of good wine unless it is a Muslim household, or flowers for wealthy hosts, or otherwise something edible. In business, the practice of giving a gift is virtually unheard of and may be considered a bribe.

Sudan

ⓘ **Currency**	Sudanese pound (SDG), SDG; SDG I = 100 qirsh	
🏨 **Hotels**	Porter SDGI–3; Chambermaid SDGI–3	
🍽 **Restaurants**	Round up	
🚕 **Taxis**	Round up	

The Republic of Sudan has a finely developed tipping culture, and a bellboy in a five-star **hotel**, for example, would certainly expect a much higher tip than similar service personnel in a two-star establishment. If you tip your porter SDGI–3 in an upmarket hotel and around a pound in a two-star then you will be about right. Consider about the same for your chambermaid per day. In **restaurants** it is acceptable to simply round up the bill, but make a mental note to check that it does not amount to less than 5% of the total figure. Local and tour **guides** expect to be tipped at the end of the tour. **Taxi** fares are simply rounded up to the nearest Sudanese pound.

Etiquette in Sudan can vary between communities. In the north, for example, the population is mainly Muslim, while elsewhere Christianity and Animism are followed so what is considered correct can differ. Alcohol as a gift is probably best avoided. Instead, go for pastries or expensive chocolate, which will always be gratefully accepted. Do shake hands, but if you are meeting someone of the opposite sex it is safer to allow them to initiate such a greeting.

Swaziland

🪙 **Currency**	Lilangeni (singular), emalangeni (plural) (E), SZL; E1 = 100 cents	
🛏 **Hotels**	Porter E5; Chambermaid E5	
🍴 **Restaurants**	10%	
🚗 **Taxis**	Round up	

Swaziland is like many other southern African countries in that a tipping culture has developed over time and is essentially a Western cultural import. It is not generally the norm for Swazi locals to tip, but visitors usually do. Around 10% of the total bill is the accepted rate in international **hotels** and **restaurants** where staff tend to have a higher expectation than smaller establishments such as cafés. It is best to leave your tip in cash. The lilangeni has parity with the South African rand, and it is acceptable to tip in either currency.

It has become customary to tip porters who assist with your luggage and chambermaids who have cared for your room during your stay. This should be done in cash. Around E5 per bag and per room per night respectively is about right. If staying at a safari lodge then the likelihood is that a staff tips box will be positioned at the front desk and you are invited to leave whatever amount you feel the service you have received warrants. **Taxi drivers** do not tend to expect a tip, but if they have been particularly helpful you might like to round up the fare.

Swazi people have a relaxed attitude to etiquette. There is no real tradition of holding a dinner party. People tend to simply turn up at each other's homes and expect to receive food and hospitality on the basis that it will be reciprocated one day. As a visitor you may be extended an invitation to a Swazi home, in which case you will not generally be expected to bring a gift with you; in fact it could even

Top tip

When you are out and about you will see references to the South African rand everywhere. The two currencies are fused, so prices are often given as 'R' for rand (E500 is the same as R500).

offend, as it could be perceived that you are suggesting that the family cannot provide hospitality. Always verbally greet everyone you meet; greetings are important to Swazi people. Handshakes are important too, and may continue for some time. When greeting older people it is polite to curtsey slightly, or clap your hands twice before shaking hands. In rural areas women are expected to cover their head when entering a person's home and to keep their gaze lowered.

Tanzania

🐚	**Currency**	Tanzanian shilling (TSh), TZS; TSh1 = 100 cents
🏨	**Hotels**	Porter TSh1,000; Chambermaid TSh1,000
🍴	**Restaurants**	10%
🚗	**Taxis**	Round up

In Tanzania you will be hard pushed to find someone that isn't gracious in terms of service, and because many people who work in the service industry receive nominal wages and rely on tips to boost their income, you may find yourself in need of many thousands of shillings to offer the people you meet a little something. Tipping is discretionary in Tanzania, but it is a widely accepted custom usually carried out using the local currency, US dollars, sterling or euros. Other currencies are difficult for locals to change as banks do not always carry every currency.

Hotels, **lodges** and **restaurants** tend not to add service charges, except in tourist areas, so you may like to round up your bill by about 10% or leave the equivalent in cash for your waiter or waitress. In bars, simply round up because change is almost worthless. Tips given to **guides** and chefs on tours, safari trips or

Top tip

If you engage the services of a recognised freelance guide always agree a price in advance and include the tip, but if a guide is appointed to you by the company you are travelling with then you should think about tipping as it is unlikely he or she would receive much more than a basic wage.

Kilimanjaro climbs are generally of similar proportions but are dependent on duration and the number of people in your group. You should allow at least TSh12,000– 22,000 per guide and per chef a day. On trekking trips allow more for the guides, and budget in about TSh5,000–10,000 per day for the porter who assists with your luggage. Remember these tips can be shared amongst the members of your group, and are always discretionary according to the service.

Always be aware of the social importance of formal greetings in Tanzania. It is actually considered rude to go straight into asking a question without first exchanging greetings. It is also considered bad form to show emotions in public, especially anger.

If invited to dinner or to stay with a Tanzanian family gifts will be appreciated, although they are not necessarily expected. You could also bring something from your country, or remember to send something when you return home. If you do give a gift, don't be surprised if your hosts don't thank you verbally – this doesn't meant that they don't appreciate it.

Tunisia

💰	**Currency**	Tunisian dinar (DT or د.ت), TND; DT1 = 100 millimes
🏨	**Hotels**	Porter DT2; Chambermaid DT2
🍴	**Restaurants**	10%
🚕	**Taxis**	Round up

Whilst you won't see many of the locals tipping; the country is now a top spot for travellers and, as such, the culture is changing. Nowadays, service personnel, especially those around the holiday resorts, along with taxi drivers, porters and tour guides are beginning to expect a reward for their efforts. So, if the service is good and you wish to tip, the general feeling is to go ahead as you won't offend anyone. As tipping is a relatively new idea in Tunisia there aren't really any predefined expectations, but the 10% rule tends to work a treat. You can be pretty sure there won't be a service charge added to the **hotel** or **restaurant** bill, so you'll know, in theory, that your entire gratuity will go to the staff member who has served you. To be sure, you might like to give it to him or her personally. In the case of chambermaids or porters then a dinar or two, either per day or per bag respectively, is about right. In the case of **taxis**, again the 10% guide works, or simply round up.

Tunisia is predominately a Muslim country and you should show respect for the beliefs and traditions of its people. Business in general is often conducted over mint tea, and sometimes over a meal. If invited to dine with a Tunisian household in their home don't be surprised if you find yourself in single-sex company. Always dress smartly, and take a gift of sweets or pastries. Gifts of alcohol are not usually considered appropriate, although some of the more Westernised locals may appreciate the gesture.

Uganda

🪙	**Currency**	Ugandan shilling (USh), UGX; USh1 = 100 cents
🏨	**Hotels**	Porter USh2,500; Chambermaid USh2,500
🍽	**Restaurants**	5–10%
🚗	**Taxis**	Round up

Although not necessarily standard practice, you may find some locals actively covet tips to boost their income, and the service you receive will almost always be attentive as a result. It is customary to tip waiters and waitresses in **restaurants** and **lodges** who have been friendly and helpful. Consider about 5% if the service has been satisfactory, 10% if exceptional. You will be unlikely to find a **hotel** or restaurant that has added any form of service charge to its bill, except possibly in the hardcore tourist areas, but it wise to check so that you can gauge a little more accurately how much to leave. You don't need to tip in bars unless you wish to round up. The bar may even do it for you because cents are worth next to nothing.

Tip **drivers** and **guides** if you are taking a tour/safari, plus the chef and porter who will cook and help with luggage respectively. Check with the company you are travelling with on what is fair, but certainly allow about USh10,000 a day for your guide, and similar or a little less for your chef and porter. Who and how much you tip is always discretionary, but always give it at the end of your trip.

Formal greetings are very important. Going straight into asking a question without first exchanging greetings is very impolite. Displaying emotions, especially anger, in public is also considered bad form. Should you stay with a family, use your judgement as to whether to repay their generosity with a gift such as sending them a present when you return home.

Zambia

🪙	**Currency**	Zambian kwacha (Kw), ZMK; Kw1 = 100 ngwee
🛎️	**Hotels**	Porter Kw5,000; Chambermaid Kw4,000
🍴	**Restaurants**	Service included
🚗	**Taxis**	Round up

Tipping isn't the custom in Zambia. In fact, it is frowned upon in **hotels** where a 10% service charge is added to bills by law. **Restaurants**, too, often add an automatic service charge, and no further tipping is anticipated. That said, many visitors are only too happy to offer something to someone who has shown them exceptional service, and this is acceptable if done without fuss. Small change or a maximum of 10% of the service value will always be appreciated. **Camps** work on about the same percentage, although it is always considered discretionary. They usually work on the basis that tips go into a 'pot' and are then distributed amongst the staff. How much you give depends on the service, but as a guide work on about Kw50,000, which is equivalent to around US$10, per person a day. That said, before offering any tip to anyone, it's vital that you check with the camp management how tips are dealt with. Each camp or lodge will have a clear policy on tipping: some will have a tip box for all staff, others will ask you to tip the guides separately, and tip the general staff via a general box. It is important that you don't tip after every game drive or activity. If you wish to give a personal gift to your safari guide, then do so when you're leaving the camp.

Greetings are important and should not be rushed. Be sure to exchange pleasantries before asking for assistance. If you are invited to a Zambian home for dinner, take a gift of food, a present for the children of the household, or something from your home country.

Zimbabwe

🪙	**Currency**	US dollar (US$), USD; US$1 = 100 cents (Nov 2010). Also South African rand (R), ZAR; R1 = 100 cents
🛏	**Hotels**	Porter US$1–2/R10; Chambermaid U$1–2/R10
🍴	**Restaurants**	10–15%
🚗	**Taxis**	Round up

The Zimbabwean dollar has long been the country's official currency but its instability has recently prompted the use of the US dollar. At the time of going to press the US dollar was the official currency, but it is expected that the South African rand, which is already widely used, may become the country's currency before it eventually reverts to using the Zimbabwean dollar. It is advisable to check the current currency situation before you travel. The US dollar is generally accepted in any denomination, but retailers are unlikely to accept notes of less than 10 South African rand or coins.

When visiting Zimbabwe, respect the fact that Zimbabweans tend not to tip and do not really expect it of visitors. If you have change from paying your bill in a **hotel**, **lodge** or a restaurant then you

Top tip

There is a severe shortage of small denomination notes in the country, which makes it difficult for retailers to give change. You should arm yourself with plenty of small notes or coins so you will not require change when paying bills. It is also worth noting that many places refuse to accept dirty, badly worn or damaged notes.

might like to leave it as a show of appreciation of good service, or round it up to about 10–12% of the value, or 15% absolutely maximum. Some hotels will accept other major currencies in addition to US dollars and SA rand too. In game lodges, spas and fine-dining restaurants, tips are expected. In **restaurants** there is a tendency to charge a service fee, in which case it is best not to tip. Otherwise it would be between 10% and 15% of the bill if the service has been good. In Zimbabwe, unlike South Africa, there is no tip given at all if the service was not good. Game rangers expect about US$5–10 per day, payable at the end of the trip. Other staff expect tips too; allow about US$3 per day per person for anyone who has had dealings with you such as your chamber staff, waiters and waitresses, your barman or the head porter. Sometimes this is given to the main person, often the manager or head porter, to apportion, or is put into a special tipping box. **Taxi drivers** do not generally expect to receive tips, although it is accepted and appreciated if you round up to the nearest dollar.

There is quite a traditional system of greetings in Zimbabwe. You should always wait for an older person to address you first. Before asking for what you want in a shop or restaurant, you should open with, 'Hello, how are you?' As in Zambia, you should use the three-stage handshake. First grip the other person's hand normally, then slide your hands up to grasp each other's thumbs, and then move your hand back down again to a normal shake.

If you are invited to dine with a local person, remember that it is considered impolite to refuse food or drinks. Taste it at least, with glowing thanks. Gifts are appreciated but not expected; your choice of gift will depend on how well you know your host, but something from your home country will always go down well.

Europe and Russia

Despite the fact that Europe is now a large and diverse collection of countries, tipping practices are fairly standard, although there are a few exceptions. In many countries, such as the United Kingdom and Finland, you will find that establishments in the main add between 10% and 15% to the bill automatically, although some expect you to round up or leave an amount that suits you. In countries like Denmark and Austria it isn't really necessary to tip at all. In the Baltic states the custom is just catching on and almost any amount is appreciated, while in Russia, which straddles two continents, people haven't always been relaxed about tipping but are now more accepting of the culture.

Albania

🖉	**Currency**	Albanian lek (l), ALL
🛏️	**Hotels**	Porter no tip; Chambermaid no tip
🍴	**Restaurants**	10%
🚗	**Taxis**	10%

The custom of tipping has traditionally been alien to the Albanians, but it is now more widespread. A show of appreciation for good service is always met with a smile. It is not obligatory, however. In order not to cause offence the best way is to simply round up the bill by about 10% when in a **hotel** or **restaurant**. In smaller establishments like coffee shops or **cafés**, pay your bill and then leave some loose change on the table. **Taxi drivers** will appreciate a tip, but it is not obligatory or expected, and only tip if the service has been good or you have hired the taxi for, say, a day's sightseeing. A good rule of thumb is to round up the fare by about 10%. Taxi fares tend to be inexpensive; agree a flat fare with the driver before starting the journey.

If you are invited to a business meeting or to dine with an associate or as the guest of an Albanian family, then be sure to arrive promptly. Punctuality is important in Albania. In turn, you will be treated to lavish hospitality and probably seated at the head of the table. An ideal gift to take a host would be flowers, a bottle of wine or something sweet like chocolate or baklava. Remember that Albania is one of the few countries where people nod when they disagree and shake their heads when meaning yes. A palm on the chest indicates thank you.

Austria

🖃	**Currency**	Euro (€), EUR; €1 = 100 cents
🛎	**Hotels**	Porter €2; Chambermaid €1–2
🍴	**Restaurants**	Service charge included, otherwise 10%
🚗	**Taxis**	10%

Waiting staff in **hotels** and **restaurants** are highly thought of and as such are paid a high rate. With this in mind, tipping, known as *Trinkgeld*, meaning 'money for drink', is not generally an obligation, but is often looked upon as a socially acceptable way of showing appreciation of good service. If you don't tip it is often perceived that you have not enjoyed your meal. Of course, if the service or food was not good then it is perfectly acceptable for you to leave no tip at all. If some Austrian menu prices make you

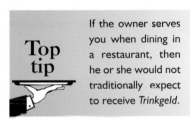

Top tip

If the owner serves you when dining in a restaurant, then he or she would not traditionally expect to receive *Trinkgeld*.

whistle, they usually include all the obligatory extras such as 10% drinking tax, 10% alcohol tax, 15% service charge, and 10% or 20% VAT. In **restaurants**, just round up the bill. When service is not included, a 10% tip is normal. Add it to the bill by advising the waiter what you wish to pay rather than leaving money on the table.

In **hotels** you'll find that porters generally expect a euro or so per bag. If they are really helpful with advice on what to see and do around the place you are staying you might like to offer a little extra. Chambermaids are likely to be looking for €1–2 per day, payable at the end of your stay, unless you're staying in a downmarket establishment. Airport porters have fixed rates. In terms of getting around, expect to offer a tip of around 10% to **taxi drivers** or simply round up to the nearest convenient figure for shorter trips, while for sightseeing **guides** offer a euro or so at the end of a short tour, more if you are on a longer tour or if the service has been particularly pleasing.

First impressions are important for Austrians, along with good manners and punctuality. If invited into an Austrian's home you should shake hands with everyone present, including any children. A small gift of chocolates or flowers – always an odd number and not red carnations, lilies or chrysanthemums – would be appreciated. Business transactions are conducted very formally in both dress and conversation.

Azores

🖉	**Currency**	Euro (€), EUR; €1 = 100 cents
🛏	**Hotels**	Porter €1; Chambermaid €1
🍴	**Restaurants**	Service charge included
🚗	**Taxis**	No tip or round up

In many respects the lifestyle in the Azores reflects that of its neighbour Portugal, with tipping being a discreet way to show appreciation of good service. Most **hotels** and **restaurants** include a service charge, but nonetheless most diners still tend to leave €1–2 on the table or offer a similar amount to the waiter directly. You may like to round up when you pay the bill, which is often a convenient way to handle the subject of gratuities. Add around €5 (or 10%) to the bill. In coffee shops and **cafés** it is OK to offer a few coins or simply allow staff to 'keep the change'. In hotels, if you have had a friendly, courteous service from a porter you may like to tip around €1 per bag. Tipping **taxi drivers** or **tour guides** is not particularly common, but if you round up the charge or offer a gratuity it will be appreciated.

The communities of the Azores are still fairly tight-knit, and simple courtesy remains important. If you are invited to dine in a local home, Azoreans will appreciate a small gift, especially if it's from your home country. Something like a good malt whisky always seems to go down well.

Belarus

🖎	**Currency**	Belarusian ruble (Br), BYR; Br1 = 100 kopeks
🛏	**Hotels**	Porter no tip; Chambermaid no tip
🍴	**Restaurants**	Service charge included
🚗	**Taxis**	Service charge included

If staying in a tourist **hotel** or dining in a **restaurant**, you can usually expect the service charge to be included, although you should make a point of checking that this is definitely the case. If not, add the usual 10% as standard, with more if you think the service has been particularly good. Similarly, if taking a **taxi** you will find a service charge forms part of the metered charge. Extra gratuities are not expected, and certainly not obligatory, but if you offer anything over and above the final bill where a service charge is already included, it will be very much appreciated. Don't simply round up a bill to, say, the nearest 100 roubles, however, because it would not represent a great deal of money. Likewise, don't be extravagant either as this may be perceived as insulting and patronising. Just offer as much as you feel the service is worth on a percentage basis. As we say, 10% is a good guide.

Dining out in Belarus tends to be for visitors and the nouveau riche only, since the average Belarusian doesn't earn nearly enough to regard doing so as anything other than a luxury. Nonetheless, if you become friendly with a Belarusian he or she will almost always invite you to their home for a meal. Acceptance on your part will be regarded as a very great honour for your hosts. Potatoes and beetroot will feature prominently as the staple ingredients of the diet, but all food will be imaginatively prepared and offered with much hospitality. Belarusians are extremely friendly people and love to chat about their country, of which they are proud. Expect to be quizzed closely about your life in your own country in return.

In business, expect protracted negotiations and always make appointments. The bureaucracy can be a bit of a minefield. Avoid offering gifts to an associate with whom you are doing business, or at least until a deal reaches a conclusion. The ideal gift for taking to someone's home is anything edible, such as traditional delicacies, sweets or biscuits from your own country, or perhaps something for the home. Chocolate in any shape or form is always an excellent and safe choice, while a bottle of vodka will be warmly received as it will mark you out as someone who has made an effort to understand the local culture. Always arrive punctually.

Belgium

🖉	**Currency**	Euro (€), EUR; €1 = 100 cents
🛏	**Hotels**	Porter €1; Chambermaid €1
🍴	**Restaurants**	Service included
🚗	**Taxis**	Round up

There's very little tipping in Belgium as all hotel and **restaurant** prices are inclusive of service charges. Of course, if you are very satisfied with a waiter's service you may want to thank him with a tip of around 5%, but it's not the custom. Waiters are highly respected and usually earn a good wage, so don't rely on tips. In a **hotel**, you may like to offer a porter an appreciation of service – around €1 per bag would be appropriate. For **taxis**, meters are structured to give the drivers a fair living and they are not dependent on tips. If the driver is particularly helpful or you're extremely happy at having

Hot chocolate

Having set off early and made such good time that we managed to catch an earlier than planned ferry at Dover for the crossing to Calais, we arrived in Bruges. I was with five friends and we were there for the Christmas market. It was a freezing cold December morning, still dark and we were desperate for a hot chocolate. A few cafés dotted around the market had still to open, although people could be seen inside. There was nothing else for it. Bang on the door, look pitiful and offer a rather large gratuity. Minutes later we were sitting in front of a roaring fire drinking hot chocolate.

Carole French

Not the pourboire

I recall my first visit to a pavement café in Ostend which normally teems during summer with short-break holidaymakers from Britain. Here, tipping customs tend to be different. I asked for my bill for a couple of drinks and some pastries. The waiter did the usual pantomime of looking skywards for divine inspiration with the maths and announced a total. I enquired, 'Service included?' He replied, 'Service included, but not the *pourboire*.' Somehow I felt cornered into rounding up the small change more generously than would a Belgian customer.

Reg Butler

found a cab when it's raining you may feel a tip is in order. Otherwise one generally rounds up the fare to the nearest 50 cents. In Antwerp, there's always great difficulty in getting a roving taxi in the pedestrianised old quarter, although you are not supposed to flag taxis down and should book in advance. Asking a café waiter to phone for one has to be worth a decent tip.

Belgium has a tradition of cementing relationships with a meal or gift. Business in Belgium is generally a formal affair, but if an associate invites you for a meal, relax, loosen your belt and enjoy it. A meal together is an important event in firming up a business relationship. Incidentally, Belgians don't like to see food wasted so finish up what's on your plate. If you visit somebody at home for a meal or drink it's customary to bring a small gift of flowers, chocolates or wine.

Bosnia & Herzegovina

🖎	**Currency**	Bosnia & Herzegovina convertible mark (KM), BAM; KM1 = 100 feninga
🛏️	**Hotels**	Porter KM2; Chambermaid KM2
🍴	**Restaurants**	10%
🚗	**Taxis**	Round up

An unsettled economy provides little help to **hotel** and **restaurant** waiters and other service personnel, and as such they earn little. The price quoted on the menu/bill will not include a gratuity. Adding 10% will barely make a dent in your budget, but it will be gratefully received. Try to leave coins rather than rounding up the bill so you know the waiter who has served you will be the one to benefit. Of course, if you receive poor or unhelpful service then there is no reason to offer anything. For hotel porters consider around KM2 per bag as a tip, and for chambermaids about the same per day. You will probably find that **taxi drivers** take the initiative and simply round up the fare themselves without consulting you, and although you may feel a little aggrieved, the reality is that the figure is likely to be so little as to not warrant a fuss. It is your choice if you wish to offer more. Tour **guides** are tipped on how well they have looked after you, rather than on a percentage basis.

Consider it an honour to be invited to someone's home and expect a number of family members to be present. Always take a gift for the hostess. A box of biscuits and coffee (200g or 500g of coffee if you are feeling generous), or sweets and coffee would be ideal. In business, meeting tends to be informal, often conducted over a meal or a drink, with the host picking up the bill. Gifts are not necessary, but if you wish to offer a small token such as a souvenir of your country then it would be received with appreciation.

Bulgaria

✒	**Currency**	Bulgarian lev (лв), BGN; лв1 = 100 stotinki
🏨	**Hotels**	Porter лв1–2; Chambermaid лв1
🍴	**Restaurants**	10%
🚗	**Taxis**	10%

Food, drink and taxi prices may seem inexpensive to some Western visitors, but not to the locals who have a lower cost of living. Likewise, tipping percentages on bills convert into modest sums for the tourist or business traveller. When paying for your meal in a restaurant, do not say 'thank you' when paying as this implies that any change is for the person to keep. Wait for your change and then decide how much to leave your waiter. Be sure to offer it directly to the waiter rather than leaving it on the table, which is considered impolite.

It is now customary to tip 10–12% for **meals** and 10% for **taxi drivers** (more for shorter rides). Porters and bellboys are appreciative of a lev or two per bag, and a similar amount should be offered to hotel chambermaids daily, garage attendants and hairdressers. Consider more for a **tour guide** if he or she has given you an enjoyable and informative excursion. There is a toilet charge in Bulgaria and you will find that in many public loos you will be charged a small amount for using the facilities. It will be approximately 50 stotinki, so remember to keep hold of small coins when going out.

In business it is expected that a gift of a pen, wine or the offer of dinner will be reciprocated, although not necessarily immediately. Bulgaria is one of the few countries where shaking the head means 'yes', and nodding means 'no'. If dining at someone's house, take a bottle of something impressive for the host and flowers for the hostess, but note that gifts shouldn't be overly expensive. Bulgarians tend to appreciate the gesture rather than the value.

Croatia

🦪 **Currency**	Croatian kuna (kn), HRK; 1kn = 100 lipas
🏨 **Hotels**	Porter 5–10kn; Chambermaid 5kn
🍴 **Restaurants**	10%
🚗 **Taxis**	10%

Croatian **hotels** and **restaurants** rarely include a service charge and tipping of around 10% is acceptable. You will just need to consider other small services, such as porterage, which is normally tipped at around 5kn per bag. A service charge is not usually included in average-grade restaurants. Away from the main tourist trail, it's enough to do as the locals do and round up to the nearest 10kn or so. Otherwise, in major resorts which are deep in the holiday trade, waiters who are doing a good job in serving an excellent meal will expect the customary tip of 10% or sometimes even up to 15%. If you experience poor service there is no reason for you to tip at all. Bar and **café** bills should just be rounded up. **Tour guides** on

Kaput!

Don't let cabbies forget to switch on their meters. I still chortle about one time in central Zagreb when, having engaged a taxi, I reminded the driver to turn on the meter. 'It's kaput' he said. 'Sorry,' I said, stepping out of the cab, 'I never use a taxi with a meter that doesn't work.' With impatient cars honking behind him he had no option but to drive on empty and rejoin the cab line while I went to the next taxi.

Reg Butler

Top tip
A good idea is to engage a cabbie for the day if you have lots of stops to make, especially if on business. It saves time waiting for radio taxis to arrive.

excursions expect to be tipped; about 15–20kn is generally appropriate. Taxi drivers are happy with a 5–10% tip, while the locals just leave small change.

Etiquette if invited to someone's home is straightforward because Croats are relatively relaxed about formality in leisure time. Take a small gift for the hostess; chocolates are ideal. Business, however, tends to be more formal in the early stages of negotiations, and you should follow the lead of the person chairing the meeting as to whether the use of first names is accepted. No gifts are necessary; only business cards.

Cyprus (South & North)

Currency	Euro (€), EUR; €1 = 100 cents (South), New Turkish lira (TL), TRY; TL1 = 100 kurus (North)
Hotels	Porter €1 or TL2; Chambermaid €1 or TL2
Restaurants	Service included
Taxis	10%

The south of Cyprus is Greek-speaking, with the local currency being the euro and the standard of living akin to most western European countries, while the north comprises the unrecognised Turkish-speaking republic and uses the New Turkish lira. The cost of a meal or staying in a hotel in southern Cyprus is relatively inexpensive for Western travellers; even more so in northern Cyprus where costs are cheaper still.

In the south, **hotels** and **restaurants** in popular tourist resorts and towns normally include a service charge of 10–15%, which is distributed amongst staff; a further gratuity is not expected. If you have enjoyed good service you can round up the bill, which is by far the easiest way to show appreciation and not offend. The menu and bill will say if a service charge is included. **Taxi drivers** would expect a tip of around 10%, although do be sure to agree a price before setting off and clarify whether this already includes a cut for the cabbie, in which case a further gratuity would not be necessary.

In North Cyprus, again a service charge is generally added to the bill in key tourist areas. If not, tipping is customary at around 10%. In other areas restaurants appreciate a rounding up of the bill as recognition of good service.

Hotel staff such as porters and chambermaids appreciate a show of gratitude and you will probably find that showing your hand early results in exceptional service. A euro in the south and TL2 in the north per bag is about right for porters, with a similar amount for chambermaids per day of your visit.

Cypriots are very hospitable and if invited to a private home to eat, consider it an honour. Your hosts will probably have invited many members of their family and expect you to shake hands with everyone, but do take their lead and follow by example. Muslim families, for instance, do not generally shake hands with women and do not welcome the gift of alcohol, but it is a good idea to take a gift for your host. Cypriots enjoy their food and one of the best gifts you can offer is a large fancy cake, a box of pastries or chocolate. In business, Cypriots prefer to meet face-to-face and a meeting will often be lengthy with no real decisions made and will finish with a meal. It will be followed by several more meetings.

Take it slow

The key to doing business in Cyprus is to take your time. For me, it was hugely frustrating until I learnt the etiquette. More used to attending city meetings, considering the facts, making a decision with my colleagues and moving on to the next issue on the agenda, sometimes all in the space of a few minutes, trying to achieve the same in Cyprus proved a pointless exercise. Meetings will go off on tangents. Ideas will be discussed, coffee consumed and much frustration will be generated in trying to get a decision agreed. But at least the sun usually shines.

Carole French

Czech Republic

🪙	**Currency**	Currency Czech koruna (Kč), CZK; 1Kč = 100 heleru
🛎	**Hotels**	Porter 20Kč; Chambermaid 20Kč
🍴	**Restaurants**	7–10%
🚗	**Taxis**	Round up

Banks are your best bet for changing money. Try to avoid exchange offices and kiosks which, although keeping much longer hours and usually opening seven days a week, have higher commissions.

Taxi drivers in Prague have a bit of a reputation for scams, but things are improving. Be sure the meter is working if you take a taxi from the train station or airport. If you have a Czech-speaking friend meeting you ask him or her to agree the price. The target cost for the 20–25-minute trip from airport to city centre is around 400Kč. If the service is good, round up the charge or add about 5–10%.

Restaurant tipping in tourist areas or cities like Prague is quite different from that prevailing in the countryside. You may see recommendations suggesting rounding up the bill to the nearest 10Kč. The reality is that waiters in tourist areas and cities expect (and generally receive) around 10% from visitors, but locals may still be giving 5%. In **rural hotels** and **restaurants** a tip of 10% would be considered hugely generous and the bill is usually simply rounded up

Top tip

Taxis can be elusive. During the daytime, they are more prevalent and often lurk near the big hotels or at the main tourist locations. Have your destination written down in Czech to show the driver so there will be no misunderstandings.

Bourgeois custom

Back in the 1950s, on my first return to what was then Czechoslovakia as a tour manager with 36 overseas visitors, we stayed at a high-grade hotel used by visitors from east and west. Our enthusiastically communist guide impressed upon me that the 'bourgeois custom' of tipping did not exist. So, on departure, I refrained from handing out gratuities to the baggage porters. As the coach drew away, I'll never forget the scowl on their faces as they glared across at our group. Even in those days they hoped that Westerners would perk up their incomes. Today, few people forget the normal 20–40 crowns.

Reg Butler

to the nearest 10 or 100Kč. Before deciding to tip always check the menu price and the amount you have been charged. Some establishments include a service charge, but most do not. Always add the tip to your bill or hand it to the waiter personally. Don't leave it on the table; it may walk. Service standards are not outstanding, but are improving. During the communist years, tipping was frowned upon and paid a basic living wage, waiters had no economic incentive to render good service – by working slowly could thin the workload. The spread of tipping culture has helped enormously. In hotels, you might like to offer a porter around 20Kč per bag.

Greetings are used everywhere – whether you're in an office, shop, restaurant or train   and a simple *'dobrý den'* ('hello', 'good day', 'good morning') or *'na shledanou'* ('goodbye') can make all the difference to the service you receive. If invited to a Czech's home for a meal, take a small gift like a bottle of wine or a box of chocolates. Bringing something from your home country will also be appreciated.

Denmark

✍	**Currency**	Danish krone (Kr), DKK; I Kr = 100 øre
♨	**Hotels**	Porter 5Kr; Chambermaid 5Kr
¶¶	**Restaurants**	Service included
🚗	**Taxis**	Service included

While the custom of tipping is known to the worldly Danish, it is not considered the traditional way of doing things in Denmark. **Hotel** bills, **restaurant** menus and the price you pay for taking a **taxi** ride will all automatically include a service charge; it is the norm. The hotel or restaurant staff or the cabbie will not expect, or even consider, that you would wish to leave extra as a gratuity. Of course, if you have received an especially attentive and friendly service, you may like to offer one, particularly if, for instance, the taxi driver has helped you with heavy luggage. It is entirely discretionary though. Offering a gratuity to hotel porters is different, however. A tip of around 5Kr per bag is considered the norm. It is also customary to tip cloakroom attendants 2–3Kr.

The giving of gifts is widely practised in Denmark. If you are lucky enough to be invited to someone's home for a meal, always take the host a small gift. Flowers, chocolate or a nice liqueur are the best bets. Gifts in business are only ever given at the conclusion of a deal, and only then something appropriate such as a smart pen, a bottle of whisky or a corporate gift with the logo of your firm clearly etched on it. Always arrive on time.

Estonia

	Currency	Euro (€), EUR; €1 = 100 cents (from Jan 2011)
	Hotels	Porter €2; Chambermaid €2
	Restaurants	10%
	Taxis	Round up or 10%

The custom of tipping was virtually unheard of in Estonia until just a few years ago. As travellers visit Estonia they bring with them traditions from other countries and so tipping habits have been adopted. Because it is all rather new there are no rules as such, but if you tip around 10% in a **hotel** or **restaurant** for a full meal, though only if the service warrants it, then that should be about right. Do check to see if a service charge is included in your bill, as some restaurants are now introducing the practice. Coffee shop and **café** staff, **taxi drivers**, tour guides and hairdressers all expect a little something for their service. Around 10% should do the trick depending on where you are. Again, if you are happy with the experience then it is at your discretion if you wish to reward the good service. Interestingly, many foreign expat communities, in Tallinn especially, are known to make a point of not tipping as a protest at levels of poor service in some restaurants. If taking a **tour**, consider around €8 for the guide for a half day or €16 for a full day.

Etiquette in Estonia is quite well defined. Punctuality is expected – you run the risk of offending if you do not phone ahead if you are going to be unexpectedly late. Dress and greetings are a tad formal. Estonians are very loyal and when a relationship has been cemented they relax a little more. Business gifts tend to be unnecessary, but if dining in a private home always take the host or hostess an indulgent but not overly expensive gift. Chocolate is always safe.

Faroe Islands

🖎	**Currency**	Faroese króna (Kr), equivalent to Danish krone, DKK; 1Kr = 100 øre
🛏️	**Hotels**	Porter 5Kr; Chambermaid 5Kr
🍴	**Restaurants**	Service included
🚗	**Taxis**	Service included

The 18 Faroe Islands are a self-governing region of Denmark. As such, the region has its own currency, the Faroese króna, which is valued alongside the Danish krone. Both are widely accepted in hotels, restaurants and when out and about.

It has never been a traditional custom in the Faroe Islands to tip for a service, and any gratuity is already built into the price you would pay for a **hotel** stay, a meal in a **restaurant** or **café**, drinks in bars or on any form of transport you may take, including **taxis**. That said, as the Faroese people have become more travelled and an increasing number of visitors have spent holidays on the islands, the practice of tipping has become widespread. It is not obligatory and is never expected, but if you wish to tip then it will not be taken as an insult. In terms of how much, it is best to use discretion. The golden rule of offering 10% is a good guide to follow.

Socialising is a largely casual affair, with friends dropping in on one another rather than making big, lavish plans to dine at somewhere exotic. If you are invited to dine in someone's home, then do take a small gift of wine or a liqueur. Chocolates, too, are always appreciated. In business, gifts should only ever be of a corporate nature, or perhaps a nice bottle of whisky, but only when you have established a relationship with the person or his or her company. The Faroese people are smart in dress and appreciate punctuality, so if you want to impress, be sure to pack a smart outfit and a watch.

Finland

♿ **Currency**	Euro (€), EUR; €1 = 100 cents
🛏 **Hotels**	Porter €1–2, Chambermaid no tip
🍴 **Restaurants**	Service included
🚗 **Taxis**	Service included

The custom of tipping is somewhat alien to the Finnish, although the practice is becoming more prevalent. Service charges are almost always included in **hotel** and **restaurant** bills, and (unusually) in the price you pay for a **taxi** ride too. No further gratuity is expected, but if you feel the service has been especially good then offering a tip will not be considered offensive. The easiest way in a restaurant, or when taking a taxi, is to round up the bill rather than to hand over money. No-one really worries if that equates to 10% or more. If you are dining with a host, leave the tip to his or her discretion.

It is acceptable to offer porters and bellboys €1 or so per bag, and even taxi drivers if they assist with luggage. Cloakroom and doormen are generally given a standard fee for their services, which is displayed in the establishment; it is usually around €2. Chambermaids do not generally expect a gratuity, but a show of appreciation for attentive service would not go amiss.

Being invited to share a sauna is an honour. Saunas are a serious matter – even business meetings are held in them. When accepting an invitation to dinner, be sure to arrive on time; punctuality is important. Take a gift of wine, flowers (avoiding white and yellow ones which are funeral colours) or chocolates for the host when dining in someone's home. Gifts tend not to be given in a business situation unless a deal is closed, then it's cognac or liqueurs, books, art or traditional local crafts. If dining out, the person making the invitation is expected to pay. Reciprocate later, rather than split the bill.

France

🖃	**Currency**	Euro (€), EUR; €1 = 100 cents
🏨	**Hotels**	Porter €1–1.50; Chambermaid €1.50
🍽	**Restaurants**	Service charge included
🚗	**Taxis**	10%

Service, normally at 15%, is automatically included in **restaurant** bills and shown by the letters 'stc' or the words '*service compris*'. This is required by law as tips are assessed for taxation. There is no need to scatter further gratuities; however, tipping is widely practised if the service is good. An accepted rate would be to round up the bill, or if inappropriate, to leave a small percentage, say 3%. Some **eateries** do not include a service charge for various reasons. Look out for '*service non compris*'. If this is the case then you are free to reward good service however you see fit. Around 15% is a good guide, 10% or less if the service was acceptable but average. For service in **cafés** and bars, small change is fine.

When paying a **hotel restaurant** bill it's optional but normal to leave cash for the waiter, depending on how you feel about quality of service. The tip would probably just be the small change, or

Top tip

If you're cruising the French waterways aboard a hotel barge you should find the cost includes gratuities for baggage handling, and perhaps for local guides and excursions. To show appreciation for on-board service, you may like to leave an overall 5% of the cruise cost as a gratuity. This is generally divided equally among crew members, including the captain.

French fashion

I had always found the French to be sticklers for punctuality, so when I was in Paris on a research trip and running late for a business meeting I was feeling flustered to say the least. The Avenue de l'Opèra seemed to be much longer than I had remembered it. I eventually arrived at my destination, glanced at the clock with a few minutes to spare, took a few deep breaths to regain my composure and announced my arrival – only to be told that the monsieur I was due to meet would arrive in ten minutes. He will, I was told with the faint hint of a smile, be 'fashionably late'.

Carole French

maybe 5–10% of the bill in pricey establishments. You can also take the easier option and round up the bill, which is always welcomed.

Service charges are not included in **hotel** bills; the price quoted to you will be the price you pay and so you may like to tip to show appreciation for a special service. For instance, you may like to tip the chambermaid at the rate of around €1.50 per day during an average three-day stay, although you will only really be expected to do so if you are staying in a hotel with rooms above €150 per night. For porters consider around €1–1.50 per bag. If the concierge or any other staff member has been especially helpful, they probably deserve recognition too.

Porters at airports or railway stations usually get a standard €1–1.50 per bag; **taxi drivers** expect around 10% of the metered fare, although rounding up is OK. Likewise, hairdressers and beauticians expect 10% of the bill. When out sightseeing, you may wish to tip museum **tour guides** if the service has been good. Around €1–1.50 tends to be the norm. It's also standard to tip excursion guides and bus drivers at around €1.50 per person, depending upon the length of the tour. Leave loose change for cloakroom attendants.

If you're entertaining business associates, you may feel it's worth tipping the maître d' at dinner shows to reserve good front seats rather than those at tables further back. Your guests will be duly impressed. The maître d' will almost certainly bestow extra attention on you and your guests too. Gifts are generally inappropriate in a business situation, because the French like to retain a sense of formality in business. In someone's home, however, a gift for the host and hostess is welcomed. A particularly good bottle of wine is always appreciated, but avoid flowers because many have associations, such as illness.

Suffer? Moi?

There are two sides to this question of tipping. I'll always recall the smallest ever group from my tour manager days. We were using the best available luxury hotels on a three-week classic European tour, but all eight of my overseas party seemed to take pleasure in complaining about their rooms and food – starting with the group sending back their *salade niçoise* because it had olive oil on it. When I gave the head waiter the usual tip and apologised for bringing such a difficult group, he rolled his eyes and said. 'Nous sommes payés pour souffrir' – 'We are paid to suffer'.

Reg Butler

Germany

🕮	**Currency**	Euro (€), EUR; €1 = 100 cents
🛏	**Hotels**	Porter €1; Chambermaid no tip
🍴	**Restaurants**	Service included plus 5–10% tip
🚗	**Taxis**	Round up

In Germany, sufficient wages are paid to most service employees, so there should really be no need for tipping, but it still tends to be expected. Service is generally considered to be included in **restaurant** bills. Waiters tend to anticipate diners will round up the bill with tips handed to the waiter direct or he's told to keep the change. In **hotels**, a porter taking luggage to your room expects a tip of €1 per bag unless you're on a conducted coach tour which includes baggage service in the package price. It is not general practice, however, to tip a chambermaid. One euro coins are very handy for other minor services, such as room service and hairdressers. Tip airport porters €1 per bag. For **taxi drivers**, it is normal to round up the fare. All tips are, of course, discretionary.

> ## Top tip
> Keep change for the cloakroom; you may find there is a fixed charge to use the cloakroom service, but if you see a plate then a gratuity is entirely voluntary.

No tipping is necessary on short rides aboard **sightseeing boats** that cruise the Rhine and Mosel (Moselle) on fixed schedules, although it is expected on any of the **package cruises** lasting up to a week. Programmes usually feature shore excursions, mostly by local **coach drivers** and **guides** who will expect a euro or two each. At the end of the cruise, there's the crew and tour director to consider.

Several operator lines running package cruises arrange a gala dinner with entertainment on the final night of the cruise, concluding with a farewell speech. The cruise or tour director will probably explain that an envelope awaits in your cabin for optional tips to be left at the front desk. The total is then equally divided among the entire crew, including the captain.

Top tip

Gifts do not really have a place in German business etiquette, but taking something for your hostess if invited to dine is appropriate. A good wine or a box of handmade chocolates from one of the many café-bakeries would work a treat.

Greece

🖳	**Currency**	Euro (€), EUR; €1 = 100 cents
🛏	**Hotels**	Porter €1; Chambermaid €1
🍴	**Restaurants**	Service charge included, otherwise 10–15%
🚗	**Taxis**	Service included

If invited to a **restaurant** it is customary for your host to pay the bill and any gratuity he or she feels is appropriate. In other circumstances, when you are dining independently for example, check whether the service charge is included in the price before deciding whether to tip, and how much. Some **hotels** and **restaurants** do include a charge, others do not. If it is included, you may like to round up the bill or leave a few euros on the plate or in the small glass in which your bill was presented to you. If a service charge is not included, and you have received good service, then reward this by offering your waiter around 10–15% of the value of the bill. You can leave it on the plate or offer it to him or her personally.

Top tip

In rural areas restaurants may add a small charge, usually referred to as a bread charge, to the bill, but you may also wish to round up as an extra gratuity.

Other people you may come into contact with and who you might like to reward for good service are **taxi drivers**, who can actually be pretty put out if you don't tip, especially if they have helped you with your luggage or offered information. It is also customary to tip cloakroom attendants, who will welcome a few coins for their service.

Known the world over for their friendliness, hospitality and business acumen, the Greeks tend to be a pleasure to socialise or work with. If you are invited to dine before, after or as part of a business meeting then it will almost always be a convivial and memorable experience. Similarly, if you are invited to someone's home you can expect to be treated as an honourable guest and be surrounded by all members of the family who will be keen to meet you. Always take your host a gift. Flowers or a nice pot plant, chocolate, wine or something traditional from your homeland would be welcomed. Dress smart casual unless the invitation is to dine at a top-notch restaurant, and don't be too worried about arriving on time. In fact, it is good form to arrive half an hour or so after the expected time, although you need to balance the traditional with not keeping your hosts waiting.

Hungary

🌀	**Currency**	Hungarian forint (Ft), HUF
🛏	**Hotels**	Porter 200Ft; Chambermaid 200Ft
🍴	**Restaurants**	10%
🚗	**Taxis**	10%

Unlike in neighbouring Slovakia and Czech Republic, tipping is a deeply entrenched custom in Hungary. Furthermore, it doesn't only apply to the hotel, catering, taxi and sightseeing sectors – the practice extends to almost everywhere that a service is rendered. At the numerous Budapest **spas**, you should tip the locker attendants around 50Ft and masseurs 200Ft. In **hotels**, porters will expect

Then and now

In my tour manager days, I took groups of visitors to Hungary during the summer of 1956, the historic year which ended with revolution. Our company boss was a Hungarian who had migrated to the UK pre-war. He said there was no point in tipping as the shops were empty, but some Western products were more highly regarded than cash. So, *en route* across Germany, I stocked up with Rotbart razor blades. At my hotel in Budapest I gave porters and waiters the tip choice: cash or blades? Without hesitation they went for the blades. From then on, we always had fabulous smiling service as all the staff knew that my pockets were swollen with packets of five high-quality safety blades...

Reg Butler

200Ft per bag. At a petrol filling station, the employee who checks your tyres or cleans your windows normally gets a small tip. At a theatre or concert hall, cloakroom staff should be tipped 100–200Ft when you hand in your coat, with the going rate sometimes posted on the wall. Among the local residents, trade staff like plumbers and electricians will often be tipped. In **restaurants**, check to see if a service charge has been added to your bill; if it hasn't, a standard tip of between 10% and 15% is expected. If you give less, or nothing, it indicates that you were dissatisfied with the service.

Budapest has an excellent public-transport system, and this is a cheaper way of navigating the city than by taxi. Note that Budapest **taxis** have a deserved reputation for overcharging unwary tourists; to protect yourself against this, it is best to order a taxi by telephone and request an estimate of the fare in advance rather than simply hailing one in the street. If you must hail a taxi, be sure that the car is marked with a name on the outside and has a yellow licence plate

How to give the tip? Cash is strongly preferred. Credit cards are not always accepted in **restaurants**, particularly outside the capital; even if you pay for your food on your card, the waiter will prefer cash for the tip itself. When your waiter brings the bill, tell him how much you'd like to pay. In other words, the cost of the meal plus however much you wish to tip. If you have the exact money just say 'thank you' as you pass over the total payment to indicate that you don't want any change. Alternatively, say nothing as you hand over payment and, when the change comes, hand your waiter the cash tip direct. Leaving the cash tip on the table as you leave is considered rude.

Top tip

During the communist period, dentists, doctors and nurses were poorly paid and it became normal for grateful patients to pay them a gratuity. Although this remains common practice among locals today, it is not expected that you as a visitor will tip anyone in the medical profession.

Top tip

as required by law. Always check that the meter is visible and re-set. Try to avoid jumping into a taxi waiting outside the big hotels as these usually charge the highest tariffs. You should tip 10%, or round the payment up to the nearest convenient figure (assuming that allows a decent enough tip). Remember that taxi drivers may not be able to change large currency bills.

When visiting a Hungarian family, take a bottle of good Hungarian wine with you – a fine Tokaji is always well received – and perhaps some flowers or chocolates. Business etiquette is similar to that in Western Europe and the U.S. The standard greeting is a handshake, and business cards are exchanged. Giving a token gift is common practice.

Iceland

🖃 **Currency**	Iceland króna (kr), ISK; 1 kr = 100 aurar
🛏 **Hotels**	Porter no tip; Chambermaid no tip
🍴 **Restaurants**	Service charge included
🚗 **Taxis**	Service charge included

Icelanders pride themselves on their good service but would never think to expect a tip – it is unheard of in Iceland. You will find that a service charge is automatically included in all bills, whether they're for services rendered in a **hotel**, a **restaurant** or when taking a **cab**. As such, there is no need to offer any further gratuity, and some personnel and owners of establishments may even take offence if you do. (As a visitor you may be excused though.) If you have received exceptional service and you really feel that you would like to show appreciation then by all means offer a gratuity; rounding up a bill is a good, diplomatic way of doing so. The rare exception to the tipping custom is if you take a specialist tour, such as a supervised trek or a fishing expedition, and then a 4,000–5,000kr tip for your **guide** would be appropriate, depending on the duration of the trip.

Business is considered important, although often appears to the visitor as being rather informal. First names are generally used, but if meeting someone for the first time it is wise to use the surname to start with as you will probably find first names become used in conversation quickly. Icelanders are keen on making informal, unannounced visits, and appointments aren't always necessary.

If you get on well with someone you are very likely to be invited to their home to eat rather than to a restaurant. It is polite to remove your shoes when entering a home, and to take a small gift for the host. Seasonal flowers are ideal. The giving of gifts in business is acceptable, but only on conclusion of a deal.

Republic of Ireland

(for Northern Ireland, see *United Kingdom*, page 112)

🏛 **Currency**	Euro (€), EUR; €1 = 100 cents	
🛎 **Hotels**	Porter €2–4; Chambermaid €2–4	
🍴 **Restaurants**	Service charge included, otherwise round up	
🚗 **Taxis**	Service charge included	

While a few euros will rarely be refused if you offer them for exceptional service, tips are not really the way of life in Ireland and are not expected.

Traditionally, service charges of 10–15% are applied to most bills. This is certainly the case in **hotels**, although a few euros to the porter who carries your bags, the chambermaid who ensures your room is always spotless and to the waiter who delivers your room service meal would not be inappropriate. In **restaurants** a service charge usually forms part of the bill, although not always. Check the menu and bill for statements that indicate whether a service charge will be added to the price or is already included. If neither of these appears then you can be sure that no charge has been made, in which case if you have received good service you might like to round up the bill or add 10% or so. If unsure, and it can be confusing, ask the proprietor– he or she will no doubt put you right. In **pubs**, which you'll find on what seems like every street corner in Ireland, never offer a gratuity. It would be considered impolite. Instead, if you are feeling generous and the service has been good the simplest way is to invite the member of staff to have a drink on you and pay accordingly.

Getting around Ireland is a straightforward business, and if you take a **taxi** then you should find the quoted price includes a little something for the driver. If you offer more though, perhaps a few euros, or around 10% of the charge for exceptional service, then it is unlikely to be refused. Other people you come into contact with who may expect a gratuity are hairdressers and barbers. Again, 10% of the bill should do the trick – give it personally.

In business, it is unusual to exchange gifts, although small tokens, such as a nice pen or item of stationery, may be offered at the conclusion of a deal. Flowers, not red and white ones or lilies, should be given to the hostess if invited to dine at someone's home. Chocolates, too, are a good choice, as is wine. Sending a thank you note after a meal is always appreciated. Remember never to decline a drink, except perhaps on medical grounds, and always reciprocate.

Italy

✎	**Currency**	Euro (€), EUR; €1 = 100 cents
⊨	**Hotels**	Porter €1–2; Chambermaid €1
⌇	**Restaurants**	10%
🚗	**Taxis**	10%

In Italy, the basics for transport and accommodation are fairly standard with airport and railway porters charging a set fee. **Taxi drivers** don't really expect a tip but about 10% is OK if they have been especially helpful, while **hotel** porters look for €1–2 depending on how many bags you have and the grade of the establishment. You may also like to give small change if a doorman calls a cab for you.

In **restaurants**, a service charge is built into the charging structure, one way or another. Either a service percentage is built into the price of each item on the menu or there's an outright *servizio* added to the bill. Alternatively, you may note there's something mysterious called '*pane e coperto*', which is a bread and cover charge. It pays for the bread, the tablecloth and the place setting. Whichever way it's structured, do as the Romans do and don't go in for over-the-top tipping, except maybe in an expensive establishment. Nothing further is needed unless you'd like to let the waiter keep the change. Most Italians themselves don't tip in restaurants and find it irritating when visiting places like America where 15–20% is customary.

A small tipping convention is well established in **snack and coffee bars**, where the bartender, known as a *barista*, and his espresso machine are the focus. You can choose to have your coffee or snack standing at the bar   the custom is normally to pay first at the cash desk (*cassa*); take the receipt to the counter, put a small coin

Top tip

In snack and coffee bars, standing at the bar is always much cheaper than having drinks and sandwiches served to a table, and you're not supposed to buck the system by ordering at the bar and then sitting down. You will probably receive slower service if you do.

on top and the *barista* then reads your order. The few cents' tip ensures rapid service, putting you a jump ahead of more parsimonious customers who don't sugar their receipt with a coin.

If taking an excursion, the **local city guide** is hired for a half or whole day sightseeing stint and is paid by the tour operator. Nothing further is expected, but an odd euro or two is never refused. Likewise, on a city sightseeing trip or an out-of-town excursion operated through a local travel agency – possibly booked through your hotel concierge – then a euro or two each for the **driver** and **guide** is appropriate.

Different colours and varieties of flowers have unpleasant associations in Italy, so while taking a gift for the host and hostess is appropriate when dining with a local family in their home it is safer to take chocolate or better still a bottle of especially fine wine. It is not necessary to take a gift to a business meeting; just a business card which you might like to have translated into Italian on one side. It would be appreciated.

Latvia

🖋	**Currency**	Latvian lats (Ls), LVL; Ls1 = 100 santimi
🛏	**Hotels**	Porter Ls50; Chambermaid Ls50
🍴	**Restaurants**	10%
🚕	**Taxis**	Round up

Latvians tend to be a little laid-back about the tradition of tipping. It is very much a case of if you wish to tip then do; if not then they won't get terribly upset about it. That said, although not obligatory, it is fairly common. The best way is to round up a bill or leave 10% of the bill. A good rule of thumb is always 10%. Some **hotels** and **restaurants** do include a service charge in their menu pricing, although by no means all. In Riga, the capital, you'll find VAT mentioned but rarely a service charge. It's worth checking so you can tailor your gratuity accordingly.

Other personnel you may wish to tip include porters at the rate of around Ls50 per bag, and perhaps even hairdressers and spa attendants to whom you might offer about 5% of the total bill. **Taxi drivers** are likely to appreciate a gesture, especially if they have been particularly helpful. The best way is to round up or add 10%, otherwise pay what is on the meter. If taking a tour, consider around Ls7 for the **guide** for a half day or Ls15 for a full day.

Latvians tend to give gifts to family members only, and then only for days of celebration like birthdays, but it is appropriate to give a small present to your host or hostess when socialising with them in their home. Business gifts are not really the done thing. Keep things formal and if you wish to strengthen a relationship invite your associate to dinner. Reciprocate if they take the initiative and present you with a gift.

Lithuania

⌘	**Currency**	Lithuanian litas (Lt), LTL; 1Lt = 100 centas
🛏	**Hotels**	Porter 5Lt; Chambermaid 5Lt
🍴	**Restaurants**	10%
🚗	**Taxis**	Round up

Few of the standard hotels and restaurants in Lithuania add a service charge to their menu or bill, but the more expensive and exclusive do. Nonetheless, it is rare to find a Lithuanian who will show any obvious signs of expecting a tip. As a people, they tend to be respectful and reserved. The service provided will almost always be friendly and efficient too, meaning that you will probably enjoy the experience and wish to show your appreciation anyway. You will find that the standard is around 10% in **hotels**, **restaurants** and for any staff member who has served you well in **cafés** and coffee shops. It isn't generally expected that you will tip bar staff. Charges quoted for a **taxi** will almost always include a little something for the driver, so it is very much up to your discretion if you wish to offer more. Rounding up may be a good way of rewarding efforts, and relieving your pocket of lots of loose change. It is not obligatory by any means, but if the driver has served you well then you may choose to do so. If taking a tour, consider around 35Lt for the **guide** for a half day or 70Lt for a full day.

Lithuanians are friendly and informal when you get to know them, socially and in business, although it may take a few meetings to reach this stage. Handshakes and eye-to-eye contact are the best policy until you know you have reached the hugging stage. Remember it is impolite to talk with your hands in your pockets. Gifts in business are usually unnecessary, but if you do feel you would like to offer something then wait until after a deal has been reached, and keep it

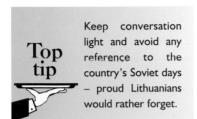

simple like wine or a pen. Hostesses like to receive flowers from guests when they entertain, but when choosing a bouquet always make sure there is an odd number and avoid white blooms, as these are only ever used for weddings. Chrysanthemums would not be a good choice either, as these are more commonly present at funerals.

Luxembourg

🏦	**Currency**	Euro (€), EUR; €1 = 100 cents
🛎	**Hotels**	Porter €1–2; Chambermaid €1–2
🍴	**Restaurants**	Service charge included
🚖	**Taxis**	Service included

Normally a service charge of 10–15% is included in the price quoted for **hotel** stays, meals in **restaurants** and for taxis, and the Luxembourgers themselves are happy to pay. That said, if you have had good service and wish to show appreciation then you will be greeted with a smile if you offer to round up the bill. While not expected, waiters and porters in top hotels are appreciative of €1–2 for their services too. If your **taxi driver** has been friendly and helpful, then you may like to add 10% or so to the meter charge. If you are taking a guided tour that lasts a few hours then a few euros for the **guide** and driver would be appropriate.

In business it is polite to arrive for your appointment punctually. If you dine, then remember that it is impolite to leave food. Only give a business gift when you are already working with a colleague or company, and not in the early stages of a relationship. Don't be surprised if colleagues invite you to partake in a cocktail before dinner and a fine brandy afterwards.

Men invariably shake hands on meeting and on leaving, as do men and women who don't know each other well. Two or three kisses on the cheek is the normal greeting among friends when at least one of them is a woman. You may be invited to a cultural event or to a private 'posh frocks' event in someone's home.

Dressing up for dinner is not essential, although some may like to anyway if it's a special occasion. Take a gift; flowers or chocolates are the norm. Wine is less common, but it won't cause offence.

Macedonia

🖂	**Currency**	Macedonian denar (ден), MKD; ден I
🛏	**Hotels**	Porter ден10–20; Chambermaid ден10–20
🍴	**Restaurants**	10%
🚗	**Taxis**	10%

The Macedonians are a hugely friendly and proud people. With an often low level of disposable income compared with some nationalities, they rarely eat out. Tipping is not common practice in **hotels** and **restaurants**, at least not by locals. Visitors, however, who may have more money to spend, may feel it appropriate to tip for good service. For a worker who may be paid a low wage, a tip can boost both the purse and the morale enormously. Offer ден10–20 for smaller priced services and then round up to the nearest ден50 or 100 on larger bills. If you go for 10% of the total then you will not be far out; any more and you could be seen as being patronising. Some restaurants and hotels have begun adding a 10% service charge to their bills, but this is rare. If unsure, do ask. As a rule though, tipping is left very much to the discretion of individuals.

Taxis are plentiful, although always hire a cab from a recognised taxi rank or by phoning a known company (most have the official five-digit number starting with 15). Individuals masquerading as taxi drivers and targeting tourists are a known concern in the country. Always secure a price before you travel and establish whether there's something in it for the driver. If not, if your cabbie serves you well a 10% gratuity would be in order.

When dining with a family in their home, arrive punctually and dress smartly. You might like to take a gift of chocolates, although the giving of gifts is not as established as it is elsewhere. Business meetings tend to be formal and the giving of gifts unnecessary.

Malta & Gozo

🖃	**Currency**	Euro (€), EUR; €1 = 100 cents
🛏	**Hotels**	Porter €2–3; Chambermaid €2–3
🍴	**Restaurants**	5–10%
🚗	**Taxis**	10%

The Maltese are a people who like to dine out and will not give a second thought to leaving a tip for good service. It is customary to leave between 5% and 10%, whether enjoying a light snack of coffee and a pastry or a full evening gourmet meal. It is perfectly acceptable to leave more if you feel the service has been extra special. **Hotels** and **restaurants** are beginning to automatically add a service charge when presenting the bill, in which case a further gratuity is not necessary. If you are unsure if a charge is included, the restaurant or hotel staff will generally be happy to help and then it's up to your discretion on whether you wish to leave more. Porters, will appreciate a few euros as a tip depending on the number of bags you have.

Taxis are readily available, too, and can be booked or hailed from ranks. Agree a route and a charge, and allow for about 10% extra to cover the tip. The quoted charge will almost always not include anything for the driver, but it's worth checking. Car parking attendants expect a few coins if assisting you. Around 15 to 25 cents should do the trick.

If travelling to Malta on business, expect a

> **Top tip**
>
> You do not need to tip bar staff unless they come specifically to your table to take the order and then serve you your drinks. A few euros is sufficient in this situation.

A gift or three

Hearing that it was customary in Malta to take a gift when accepting an invitation to dine in someone's home, but not really sure what to take, I decided upon a rather colourful selection of flowers tied with a bow, some chocolates and some wine. I headed to my hosts' home in Valletta, ensuring I was punctual. While my friends were clearly delighted with my gifts, I did sense surprise and perhaps even a little discomfort. Less is most definitely more in Malta, I found. Next time I will take flowers, nice chocolate *or* wine and avoid making my hosts feel uncomfortable.

Carole French

fairly regimented way of doing things. The Maltese, although hugely friendly, like to work in an orderly manner and you will probably find a well-organised agenda in place for meetings. Punctuality will be expected, dress should be conservative and you will probably be invited to dine afterwards. Business gifts are best left until a deal is complete. In terms of gifts, if dining in someone's home, which is a huge honour, take some flowers, chocolate or wine, or perhaps something traditional from your homeland. A gift should be about gesture, not value. Again, punctuality would be greeted with appreciation.

Montenegro

🖎 **Currency**	Euro (€), EUR; €1 = 100 cents	
🏨 **Hotels**	Porter €1–2; Chambermaid €1–2	
🍴 **Restaurants**	10–15%	
🚗 **Taxis**	10%	

A new wave of tipping culture is emerging in Montenegro. **Hotels** and **restaurants** do not generally include a service charge and therefore leaving a tip is very much at the discretion of the guest or diner. Montenegrins themselves do not tend to tip much as a general rule, preferring to round up the bill to the nearest convenient denomination. In practice, this may not amount to a very high percentage, and visitors more used to tipping may prefer to leave a little more. As a guide, by far the simplest way is to take the figure on the bill, add 10–15% and round it off to the nearest euro.

If taking a **taxi**, always agree a figure before starting your journey and clarify whether it includes something for the driver. Montenegrin taxi drivers do not tend to expect a tip, and are certainly unlikely to solicit one, but if you have received a good, friendly service and especially if your driver has gone out of his way to help you with directions or with your luggage then a 10% tip would be reasonable.

Montenegrins are hospitable by nature; if invited into a home you are likely to be offered a glass of *rakija*. When the inevitable toast is proposed, maintain eye contact with the toaster. It is customary to take a gift, with imported items being especially welcome. Women love to receive handcream, perfume or anything from your own country, but not chocolate or sweets.

The Netherlands

🖃 **Currency**	Euro (€), EUR; €1 = 100 cents
🛎 **Hotels**	Porter €1–2; Chambermaid €4
🍴 **Restaurants**	Service charge included
🚗 **Taxis**	Service charge included

While service charges are automatically included in **hotel** and **restaurant** bills and **taxi** fares in the Netherlands, tipping is, surprisingly, very much a part of life. Although not expected, tips are given to everyone from taxi and coach drivers, and airport porters right through to hotel and restaurant staff, and indeed many other service personnel you might come into contact with. That said, the Dutch will only tip a nominal sum and only then if the service has been exceptionally good. The Dutch like to feel happy and content, and do not find poor service agreeable.

A tip of a few euros is customary for **coach drivers**. **Taxi** fares are quite hefty and drivers do not expect a tip, but will appreciate a few euros, particularly if an extra service is involved, such as carrying bags. Usually rounding off the fare is sufficient; locals may opt not to pay a tip at all. In **hotels**, **restaurants** and **cafés** where a 15% service charge is automatically included it is usual to leave an additional 10%. If you feel this is a bit too generous on top of the 15%, simply round up the bill to the nearest euro. You can give the

Top tip

It is considered polite to refer to the country not as Holland but as The Netherlands. Holland is only a very small region to the west side of the country. The Netherlands is the whole of the country.

91

tip to the waiter, but it is more usual to simply leave the change or a few coins on the table. If you are only ordering drinks, it is perfectly acceptable to pay the exact amount.

For porters offer €1–2 per item of luggage, and around €4–5 per day for chambermaids. It will not be necessary for you to tip a hairdresser or barber if you plan a new look during your stay.

The giving of gifts is done with finesse in the Netherlands. Always beautifully wrapped, they are hugely appreciated if taken to a friend's or a business associate's home. Flowers are the most common gift but not lilies or chrysanthemums; these are for funerals only. Chocolates, a plant or a bottle of wine are also appreciated. In business, which is conducted in quite a formal fashion, refrain from giving gifts until after a deal has been made or you have built up a good rapport. It is polite to arrive for your appointment punctually. It will be frowned upon if you do not.

Waste not

Some years ago, having been invited to dine with some very good friends in the Netherlands, I was eagerly looking forward to a new food experience. That's exactly what I got. With a grill and a mountain of food in front of us I was told we were all going to cook our own food. OK, I thought, this will be fun. And it was. We managed to get through all the food, which, although bad for the diet, was good because it's considered very bad form to waste food in the Netherlands. I have since purchased three similar grills and 'entertained' friends in a similar manner – although now have a reputation for inviting people to dinner and not doing any cooking!

Carole French

Norway

🖉	**Currency**	Norway krone (kr), NOK; 1kr = 100 øre
🛏	**Hotels**	Porter no tip; Chambermaid no tip
🍴	**Restaurants**	Service charge included
🚗	**Taxis**	Service charge included

The tradition of tipping is almost unheard of in Norway, although like many places around the world the expectations of service personnel are changing. You will almost always get good service, whether you tip or not. Norwegians tend to be a proud people and will not want you to be dissatisfied with the service you have received. **Hotels** and **restaurants** always include a service charge, as do the charges you would be quoted when taking a taxi. No further gratuity is expected, other than a small show of appreciation to a **taxi driver** or airport porter for assisting with luggage. Around 10kr per bag would be about right. If you do decide to leave a tip for a waiter, you can offer it directly or simply round up the bill; either is acceptable. Since the practice is rather new there are no hard and fast rules; you could take the yardstick of 10% as a guide. In a bar, locals would tend to leave 5–10kr.

Norwegians don't, as a rule, tip either chambermaids or porters. The general assumption is that by paying for a hotel room you would expect it to be clean, and bags can be carried without the help of a porter. Smaller hotels are unlikely to have porters anyway. If you wish to leave something then feel free to do so, but don't be worried if you don't.

The giving of gifts in a business environment is unnecessary, but the need to arrive punctually and dress smartly is. When visiting a person's home, flowers make an ideal gift for the hostess, although avoid white flowers which are usually used for funeral arrangements.

Poland

🦪	**Currency**	Polish złoty (zł), PLN; 1zł = 100 groszy
🏨	**Hotels**	Porter 5zł; Chambermaid 5zł
🍴	**Restaurants**	Service charge included
🚗	**Taxis**	10%

Poland plans to adopt the euro when its economy is a little healthier, but in the meantime, the currency is the złoty.

A service charge of 10% is normally automatically included in **restaurant** and **hotel** bills, but not in taxi charges. As a result, gratuities to waiting staff need only be given if the service has been good, and most will do their best to give you a good service as they need to supplement often low wages with tips. A few złotych up to 10% of the bill is about right if you have been looked after satisfactorily. The easiest way is to leave some change on the table or give it to the waiter directly to ensure he or she receives it.

Taxi drivers would usually like a tip equating to about 10% of the taxi fare, and would probably be put out if they didn't receive it. You may even find an unwillingness to help with luggage if no tip is apparent. Ultimately it's down to your discretion as to whether or not you tip and by how much, but it is considered customary to do so. Rounding up is a good idea to avoid having to deal with the fiddly

Top tip

When paying your restaurant bill, if you are expecting change from, say, a large note be wary of saying 'thank you' as it implies you mean 'keep the change'. The tip could prove larger than you had intended. Wait until you have your change and then express your thanks.

Tale of a five dollar bill

I was working in Warsaw when a friend arrived for a short visit. We tried to book him into a hotel room but were told there were none available. I fiddled with a five dollar note as we pondered what to do. Suddenly a room had become available. Nothing was said on either side, but at the exact moment the receptionist indicated a room had been found, the banknote, accidentally, slipped from my fingers. It must have been magic.

Reg Butler

little coins. In cloakrooms, expect to pay a few złotych; ditto for anyone who helps you with luggage in your hotel, although this is in no way obligatory.

In business, remember to always use the title and surname of your associate unless he or she leads by using first names, and if you are invited for a meal it would be impolite to actually talk about work, contracts, etc, until your host does. A meal is considered the time when potential working associates get to know each other. Corporate gifts should always be avoided until after a deal has been struck. If invited to dine with a Polish person in their home, always be punctual, dress smartly and take flowers, although not yellow, white or red ones, and always in odd numbers, as a gift for the hostess. Other suitable alternative gifts are pastries, chocolates or wine, but keep them modest so as not to offend.

Portugal

	Currency	Euro (€), EUR; €1 = 100 cents
	Hotels	Porter €1–2; Chambermaid €1
	Restaurants	Service charge included
	Taxis	10%

In Portugal, it's considered unrefined to give tips with other people watching. Restaurant gratuities should be given discreetly or the cash just left on the table, although it is becoming more 'upfront' in cities like Lisbon and Porto. Portuguese waiters are viewed and paid as professionals. A gratuity is seen as appreciation for good service, not as a means to make up for a tiny wage. The locals usually just leave small change and don't do percentages. Otherwise, €2 around 10% is a good-value tip, especially as a service charge (*servicio*) is usually added to a **hotel** or **restaurant** bill. At a bar, bakery or **café**, loose change is enough. At your hotel, tip €1 or €2 if a porter brings luggage to your room. You could also consider a daily euro for the chambermaid and €1 each time anyone provides extra service, like bringing breakfast to the room.

You may find that **taxi drivers** do not speak English, French or German. Ask your hotel doorman to tell him your destination, or have it written down. Most taxis are metered and also display approved extras for weekend, bank holiday and late-night services, plus a baggage surcharge to and from airports. Small change or up to 10% of the fare is a normal gratuity. To hire a car and driver for the day or longer, ask your concierge to negotiate the fee. Ideally get the agreed details in writing. Any end-of-trip gratuity should be at your discretion depending on how helpful the driver has been. As regards tipping other service personnel, such as hairdressers and cloakroom staff, it isn't really necessary and not really the done thing.

Portugal is a popular business destination. If you are going on business it's worth taking some appropriate goodies from your own country in case you wish to reciprocate a gift as it's quite common to exchange presents with business associates. The value may depend on the company status of those you are visiting, and whether they are existing suppliers or customers. If you already know your contact's tastes and interests, coffee-table books, DVDs or good-quality foreign liqueurs may be appropriate. Gifts are normally reciprocated. When received, they should immediately be unwrapped and admired. If invited to dinner at somebody's home, the hostess will welcome chocolates or toys for the children. Remember: white chrysanthemums are for funerals and red blossoms symbolise revolution. It's best to avoid flowers.

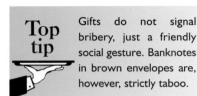

Top tip

Gifts do not signal bribery, just a friendly social gesture. Banknotes in brown envelopes are, however, strictly taboo.

Romania

🖲	**Currency**	Romania new leu (plural lei), RON; 1 leu = 100 bani
🛏	**Hotels**	Porter 5 lei; Chambermaid 5 lei
🍴	**Restaurants**	Service charge included
🚗	**Taxis**	5–10%

If you are wanting to exchange money on arrival in Romania the best way is to look out for the '*casa de schimb*' or the '*birou de schimb valutar*', which are authorised exchange offices, although there are also ATMs. Banks will change money for you too, giving the best rates, and, of course, they are 100% reliable.

Romania is fast becoming a popular holiday destination and represents good value to Western travellers when compared with many other destinations. A service charge is generally included in **hotel** and **restaurant** bills as a matter of course, and these days tipping is expected. A basic guide would be 5–10% of the bill as a tip for waiting staff. A similar amount would be appropriate for **taxi drivers**, hairdressers and any serving staff you may meet such as in a **café**.

Traditional gifts like chocolates and wine are suitable if you are invited to a Romanian's home to eat, or coffee would be much appreciated, as are toys or sweets in smart wrappings if your host or hostess has children.

Take the lead from your business associates in the matter of gifts, as the age-old feeling of uncertainty over what is a bribe and what isn't is often deep-rooted in Romanian culture.

Russia

⬮	**Currency**	Russian ruble (руб), RUB; руб= 100 kopeks
🛏	**Hotels**	Porter руб30; Chambermaid руб30
🍴	**Restaurants**	7–15%
🚗	**Taxis**	Round up

Straddling two continents, Russia is becoming a little more relaxed about tipping, known as *chayeviye*, which in Soviet days was not so widely acceptable. Even as recent as ten or so years ago, accepting gratuities was discouraged. As a result, the culture has never really been one of providing a warm and friendly service. No matter how much waiters enjoyed their work, or how well they got on with their customers, there was no real incentive to 'go the extra mile'. Things are changing, and tipping has become a little more widespread, although it still remains discretionary. In **hotels**, especially those in major cities like Moscow and St Petersburg which see a regular number of businessmen and women from around the world, the expected level of tipping is not unlike those found in similar Western establishments. Porters are likely to expect a few rubles per item of luggage – in smaller hotels and most **restaurants** the tips are generally much less than might be expected in other countries, and in rural areas tipping is still not largely the done thing.

As a guide, look at rounding up to the nearest 20 rubles or so, or adding an additional 7–10% in a mid-range venue, or if an upmarket place about 10–15%. Because the overall bill is likely to be less, then so the tip percentage equates to a modest amount when compared to other countries. Do watch out for service charges though. Some hotels and restaurants do include one, although not all. Of course, if the service is poor then there is still no reason to tip at all.

It is not customary to tip in **cafés** or coffee shops, but it is in nightclubs and to cloakroom attendants. It is also becoming so for **taxi drivers** too, despite the fact that the price quoted for the cab will probably already include a personal cut. Do agree a price before travelling, and if you wish to offer a gratuity, even though there is no obligation to do so, round up or add about 10%. Tour **guides** tend to expect around 10% of the value of the tour, be it two hours or two days in duration.

Gifts are given with a flourish, in both social and business circles. Wine, vodka or flowers, only in odd numbers, make great gifts if accepting an invitation to dine in someone's own home, but you could opt for something completely different like perfume, an ornament for the home or toys for the children. A craft item from your homeland always goes down a treat too. In business, it is polite to socialise a bit and get to know each other before discussing corporate matters.

Serbia

🖲	**Currency**	Serbian dinar, RSD; RSD1 = 100 para
🏨	**Hotels**	Porter RSD1,100; Chambermaid RSD1,100
🍴	**Restaurants**	10–15%
🚗	**Taxis**	Round up

Tipping, known as *napojnica* in Serbia, is somewhat alien to the Serbs, and is neither obligatory nor expected – the price you see in hotels or in restaurants has traditionally been the price you pay. However, times are changing, and the practice of tipping is becoming more widespread.

In cities like Belgrade, which sees more visitors than most other areas of the country, standards are gradually being set. It is now widely considered that adding 10–15% of the total bill in a smart **restaurant** is appropriate, while in less expensive eateries, and in bars, it is acceptable to round up the bill. You will find, too, that musicians who play in restaurants expect a small tip from diners, especially if they have played for you at your table. In hotels, porters now tend to look for around RSD1,100 per bag, and chambermaids the same for each day of your stay. **Taxi drivers** as a rule do not expect *napojnica*, but it is becoming common to round up the bill or offer that the driver keeps the change. If you take a sightseeing tour of a few hours or even a day's duration, you will not be expected to tip the driver or **guide**.

Serbians take a pride in their reputation for hospitality and, if invited to dine in a restaurant, you should expect your host to pay, regardless of their financial standing. When sharing a toast with someone, look directly into their eyes. To avoid eye contact is considered rude. If invited into someone's home, even for just a cup of coffee, to refuse could cause offence.

Gift-giving is not really expected when you visit someone, but if you are invited for a meal then taking chocolates, fancy cakes or pastries will usually go down well. Taking a bottle of wine along is considered a bit odd, as this is a wine-producing country. Books and magazines also make nice gifts if the recipients speak English, or even if they don't but the subject matter or photos relate to your own home country.

Slovakia

🖉	**Currency**	Euro (€), EUR; €1 = 100 cents
🏨	**Hotels**	Porter €1–2; Chambermaid €1–2
🍴	**Restaurants**	10%
🚗	**Taxis**	Round up

Tipping has been a part of life in Slovakia for many years. It was common practice to round up the bill to the nearest ten koruny as a tip to waiting staff, your taxi driver or the masseuse at the State-run spa because it was generally known that wages were low. Slovaks no longer follow the old rule of rounding up, now to the nearest euro, and tipping is slowly becoming more structured, especially in major towns like Bratislava, Nitra, Trnava and Presov, and spa and winter-sport resorts. Your tipping will become much easier if you learn at least some basic Slovak, with German being a good back-up.

Today, service charges of around 10–15% are firmly established in **spa resorts**, **restaurants** and **hotels** used by Western tourists and businessmen. In these hotels, baggage porters expect a euro per bag, and room service personnel a few euros apiece. Give a euro or two for a concierge who has taken time in sorting out a problem or has been especially helpful with advice on where to go and what to do. In

> **Top tip**
>
> When paying a bill in a restaurant, take care when saying 'thank you' as you hand over the banknotes as this indicates you don't want any change.

restaurants that haven't yet adopted an automatic service charge, waiters expect a 10% tip. If you pay by credit card, it's better to give the gratuity in cash. Don't just walk away from the table leaving the

It's a wrap

If you add bathing in mineral-rich underground waters, facials and massage to the unimaginably beautiful landscape and clear air of Slovakia you have a holiday or business break that will be unforgettable.

The country is famous for its spas. Try a soothing algae wrap. The sheer relaxation of the experience and the effect it has on softening and cleansing the skin will be well worth the 15% or so that therapists expect you to add as a gratuity to the bill. If you haven't come to Slovakia for a spa break, try to include at least one treatment in your itinerary.

Carole French

tip but hand it over personally to the waiter. For **taxis**, you can either let the driver keep the small change or give roughly 10% of the cost as a tip.

Slovaks are warm people and although most invitations to dine would be at a local restaurant, you are very likely to be invited to someone's home after a few meetings. Gifts for the host and hostess might include a good bottle of wine and chocolates. Flowers are welcomed, but avoid white or funeral flowers. Gifts are not generally necessary in business, although once you have established a relationship with your colleague you might like to suggest a meal, for which you would pay. Take a business card with you to meetings.

Slovenia

🖉	**Currency**	Euro (€), EUR; €1 = 100 cents
🏨	**Hotels**	Porter €1–2; Chambermaid €1–2
🍴	**Restaurants**	10%
🚗	**Taxis**	Round up

Slovenia is shaking off its erroneous reputation as an Eastern-bloc country and is now one of Europe's more popular holiday destinations. Tipping, although unheard of a few years back and neither required nor expected even today, is becoming an accepted custom, albeit slowly in some areas. Should you wish to leave a tip for good service, around 10% of the bill is becoming the norm in **restaurants** and **hotels**. If the service is not up to scratch then it is acceptable to leave nothing. When out and about, **taxi drivers** may be particularly attentive if there's the likelihood of a tip, but that's no bad thing. They are often full of useful local knowledge.

Slovenes are proud of their country and immense heritage. This is also true when meeting people socially or on business. Show respect to the country and its traditions. Remember, too, that Slovenes consider punctuality important and do not take kindly to people who are impolite. If invited to dine, always take your host a small token of appreciation. A nice piece of glassware or traditional craftwork from your homeland is especially appreciated, as is a bottle of wine. It is not necessary to offer a gift in a business situation, only your card.

Spain

🖉	**Currency**	Euro (€), EUR; €1 = 100 cents
🛏	**Hotels**	Porter €1; Chambermaid €1
🍴	**Restaurants**	Service charge included
🚕	**Taxis**	Round up

Spaniards are relaxed about tipping etiquette. In **restaurants**, a service charge of between 10% and 15% is usually included, even if it's not shown separately on the bill. Apart from just leaving small change, satisfied customers would tip a further 5–7%, or up to 10% of the total in smarter restaurants where waiters most definitely expect to be tipped. In an upmarket gourmet establishment, tipping could go up to 15%, so a lot depends on the grade of restaurant. A similar variable scale is normal for table service in bars. Either hand the tip direct to your waiter or leave the cash on the plate used for bringing the bill.

In **hotels** there's not much tipping to consider beyond the usual billing of service charge. If the bellboy sees you to your room, that means €1 per bag. Maybe €1 or so a day for room service, especially if your chambermaid is especially helpful and conscientious. You can give small change in the hotel bar too. In Spain it all tends to be discretionary.

As regards **taxis**, on arrival at the airport cabbies will charge for baggage by the piece above what the meter reads, and then a 10% tip is expected. Official rates should be displayed at airports and inside any licensed taxi. Throughout Spain, you'll find that cabs are not always metered. If there is no meter, your driver will carry a booklet of the official rates and supplements for baggage and night service set by the local town hall. This can leave an innocent tourist rather out of his or her depth, however. Try to establish a price in

Top tip

On sightseeing trips by coach, tipping is expected. The average is €1 each for the **guide** and **driver**. A bread basket usually awaits your offerings on the dashboard as you depart. The loot will then be shared.

advance and then you'll be happier about giving a tip. Taxis, it has to be said, are excellent value in Spanish city centres where parking and congestion can be a nightmare.

Beyond the folk in these catering and transport services there are few other tippings to consider. For hairdressers about 10% is normal. It depends on the situation, but tipping is never obligatory.

Spaniards like to give gifts in a leisure environment, but less so to business associates other than items like a card holder, pen or notebook emblazoned with a company emblem. If dining in a private home, take fine wine, pastries or a small gift for the children.

Sweden

🖃	**Currency**	Swedish krona (kr), SEK; 1kr = 100 öre
🛏	**Hotels**	Porter 5–10kr; Chambermaid 5–10kr
🍴	**Restaurants**	Service charge included
🚗	**Taxis**	Round up

Tipping is not traditional in Sweden, and whether you are in a **hotel**, a **restaurant** or taking a cab, you will not be expected to leave any form of gratuity. In fact, if you do it may be thought of as rather strange. People tend to pay the quoted figure or round up to the nearest 10kr, especially in taxis or restaurants. Furthermore, rounding up is more for convenience than as a form of gratuity. If a **taxi driver** is especially helpful with luggage or information, you may like to offer a few kronor as a tip to show appreciation, but otherwise it won't be expected. Porters should receive around 5–10kr per bag, and cloakroom attendants a little more.

Taking gifts to business meetings is a virtually unheard-of practice. In fact, many companies have a policy of not accepting gifts at all. Offering a gift of alcohol or something traditional to your country may be acceptable after closing a business deal, but it is discretionary. If you are given a gift then reciprocate with something of similar value. Dining in someone's home is a little different, but not much. It is not obligatory to take a gift, but if you feel better taking the host a token of your appreciation then wine, unwrapped flowers or chocolates are safe bets. Never take chrysanthemums or white lilies though, as these are for funerals only, and always be sure there are an odd number of blooms.

Switzerland

🐚 **Currency**	Swiss franc, CHF; CHF1 = 100 centimes/centisimi/rappons (depending on the sector in this multi-linguistic country)	
🛏 **Hotels**	Porter CHF3–5; Chambermaid CHF3–5	
🍴 **Restaurants**	Service charge included	
🚗 **Taxis**	Round up or 5–10%	

Service personnel receive a professional wage in Switzerland and **restaurants** and **hotels** generally incorporate a service charge of 15% into the price quoted for food and drink on the menu itself. As a result, tipping is simply not necessary or expected. That said, if you receive exemplary service, a small amount handed to a waiter personally will always be appreciated, but it is not considered an obligation. The same goes for hotel porters, to whom you may like to offer a few francs per item of luggage, and to chambermaids. Also, offering a small gratuity to **taxi drivers** who have given you particularly good service is, you might feel, appropriate. Taxi fares are usually structured so as to include a service charge, although this can vary from one district or city to another. Check if you are unsure. A little extra doesn't go amiss if you are happy to give it, but don't feel obligated.

Give exquisite chocolate, art, crafts or flowers to the hostess if you accept an invitation to dine in someone's home. The Swiss are appreciative of quality, but not of ostentatiousness, so keep your choice of gift subtle. The Swiss are not tolerant of sloppiness either, so be prompt and dress smartly. It is by far the best policy to take your business associate's lead in gift giving because Switzerland is a multicultural and multi-linguistic country and, as such, thoughts on what is acceptable as a gift and when it is given can differ.

Turkey

🖉	**Currency**	New Turkish lira (TL), TRY; TLI = 100 kurus
🛏	**Hotels**	Porter TL2; Chambermaid TL2
🍴	**Restaurants**	10%
🚗	**Taxis**	Round up

Straddling Europe and the Middle East, Turkey is accustomed to both the traditional custom of *baksheesh*, which is optional and given in modest sums only, and the tipping practices of Westerners on luxury holidays. Where once a tip would have been given for good service, now it is often expected. Nonetheless, if you receive poor service you should not feel obliged to leave a tip.

As a guide, give around 5–10% of the value of the bill in a **restaurant** or **hotel**. Tipping is usually done by rounding up the bill or by suggesting that the waiting staff keep the change. In hotels, if a porter obliges by assisting with your luggage then around TL2 per bag is always appreciated. **Taxi drivers** do not expect to be tipped, but rounding up the bill will be appreciated. Other service personnel who you might like to reward are **tour guides**, especially if it is a private tour, in which case offer around TL10–15, as well the staff in a Turkish bath (*hammam*). Allow around 10% of the price you paid for the bath.

It's virtually unheard of to give gifts in a business environment. If you wish to cement a relationship, extend an invitation to dinner instead – as the host, you will be expected to pay. If you are invited to dine in a private home, take pastries, chocolate, or perhaps toys if your host or hostess has children. Avoid alcohol unless you are sure your host would not be offended – Turkey is a Muslim country.

Ukraine

💰	**Currency**	Ukrainian hryvnia (sometimes the hryvna or grivna), UAH; UAH1 = 100 kopiyka
🛏	**Hotels**	Porter UAH8–10; Chambermaid UAH8–10
🍴	**Restaurants**	10–15%
🚗	**Taxis**	10%

Ukraine has transformed itself from its Soviet days and has become a popular travellers' destination. The downside of this is that where once tipping wasn't a traditional practice (you would have been hard pushed to convince a Ukrainian that they should take extra money from you) it would now appear they are beginning to think that tourists will tip for anything, regardless of the quality of the service or food. So while a tip may be expected, if the service has been poor then there is no reason to feel obliged to tip. It really is a matter of personal judgement.

As a guide, check to see if a service charge has been included in the price you are being billed in a **hotel** or **restaurant**, which is unlikely unless you are in a mid- to top-end establishment, and then add 10% as a tip if your experience has been pleasurable. If it has been exceptional then 15% is regarded as the going rate. **Taxi drivers** don't really expect anything; they take a pride in their work and will provide a service irrespective of whether you tip. However, you will have to agree a price beforehand. If you round up or add about 10% to the bill, you will no doubt find they will thank you graciously.

When entering someone's home, take off your shoes near the entrance; normally you will be offered slippers to wear. If you have been invited to dine, take a small gift from your own country or flowers. If you completely empty your plate, it will be refilled. Refusing a drink is considered very rude.

United Kingdom
(including Northern Ireland)

🐚	**Currency**	British pound (£), GBP; £1 = 100 pence
🛏	**Hotels**	Porter £1–2; Chambermaid £1–2
🍴	**Restaurants**	Service charge included, otherwise 10%
🚕	**Taxis**	Round up

The British tend to be straightforward about things. If they hire someone to do a job and they have been quoted a fair price for the work then they expect it to be done well with no further expenses added. Rounding up a bill or adding a gratuity to, say, a restaurant bill would be considered a personal choice and, irrespective of whether fellow diners wish to leave a tip, you are under no obligation to do so. That said, it is a nice gesture to add a little something if the service has been good, and tipping is widespread. Do bear in mind that many hotels and restaurants include a service charge in their pricing. A good guide for tipping **hotel** and **restaurant** staff, **coach drivers**, **taxi drivers** (especially black-cab drivers in London) and hairdressers is between 10% and 15%, the latter only for exceptional service.

There is no real reason to tip bar staff, but if you have built up a rapport with the barman or barmaid then you might like to offer them a drink, otherwise don't worry. Similarly you may like to offer a tip to a take-away delivery person, which is, in general, common practice. There is no real reason to tip

> **Top tip**
> The British don't like a 'big show', so the best way to tip is to round up the bill, or in a restaurant leave it quietly on the plate or table.

anyone else you meet, and certainly not the police or other public service personnel; in the case of police it could be construed as bribery. Some private members' clubs and companies forbid their employees from taking tips too.

In terms of gifts, taking flowers, chocolates or wine is considered good form when accepting an invitation to dinner in someone's home, or if attending a garden party or barbecue.

In business the giving of corporate-style gifts tends to come when a relationship has passed the initial stages and deals or contracts have been reached. Typically, gifts might include a fine whisky, wine, desk items and pens, and are often given at Christmas. If you are invited to dinner, then it is appreciated if you reciprocate at a subsequent meeting.

Middle East

It is standard practice to tip in most Middle Eastern countries, although the amount is generally considered to be discretionary. In Bahrain, for example, it is customary to tip most service personnel. In some of the finer hotels and restaurants, such as those in Dubai, you may find a service charge of between 10% and 15% added to your bill. In Iran, Oman and Jordan, even if a charge appears on your bill, it is often good practice to offer a further gratuity.

Bahrain

🖎	**Currency**	Bahraini Dinar (د.ب. or BD), BHD; BD1 = 1,000 fils
🏨	**Hotels**	Porter 250 fils; Chambermaid 250 fils
🍴	**Restaurants**	10%–15%
🚗	**Taxis**	Round up or 10%

Bahrain is a wonderful place to visit and its service personnel are usually extremely efficient and friendly. Most **hotels** will add a service charge of 10%, but as you will almost certainly be treated well by the porters and chamber staff you might like to consider leaving a little extra to these staff as a tip. For porters offer around 250 fils per bag, and 250 fils per day to chambermaids. In **restaurants**, your bill will state whether a service charge is included, and if it is it will be between 10% and 15%. This amount is designed to be shared amongst staff. If the waiting staff have been particularly attentive, then they will appreciate you leaving a little more for them. Work on 10% of the price you paid for your meal.

Taking a **taxi** or an **organised tour** is one of the best ways to visit the sights of Bahrain. In the case of a taxi, always take a metered taxi cab and if your driver has been helpful then round up the fare to about 10% as his tip. For tour guides and drivers allow around 10% of the price you paid for your excursion.

Bahrainis are hospitable and if you strike up a friendship you will almost certainly be honoured with an invite to the person's home. Expect lots of family members. Dress well for your visit, arrive punctually and take a gift of confectionery for your host which you should offer with both hands. Gifts in a business situation are unnecessary, but you should arrive at a meeting at the stated time and present your business card.

Iran

🖎	**Currency**	Iranian rial, IRR; I rial = 100 dinars
🛏	**Hotels**	Porter 3,000 rials; Chambermaid 3,000 rials
🍴	**Restaurants**	Service charge included, otherwise 5–10%
🚗	**Taxis**	Round up

The amount quoted in **hotels** and **restaurants** generally includes a service charge, but additional gratuities are appreciated as wages tend to be low and inflation high. Around 5–10% is appropriate. Many of Iran's restaurants have separate areas: one for women and children and the other for men.

Tipping airport porters is customary. About 5,000 rials is about right. Hotel porters are generally happy with around 3,000 rials per item of luggage. Cloakroom attendants look for around 1,000 rials while tour or attraction **guides** expect about 5,000 rials. For **taxi drivers**, it is best to agree a price before setting off. Your driver will assume this does not include a tip, so you may wish to offer 10% or round up. It will always be received gratefully.

If visiting a family home, shoes should be removed on arrival, but feet must remain covered with socks or tights. Arrive punctually, take a small, wrapped gift such as pastries, and be prepared for the fact that you may be dining in single-sex groups. Do not shake hands. Do praise the house, food or hospitality, but never a household item, otherwise it will be given to you.

Doing business in Iran is formal and so you should always meet by appointment, dress smartly and be punctual. Business gifts are unnecessary, but it is advisable to take a business card with you to your meeting and have one side translated into the local language.

Israel

💱	**Currency**	New Israeli Shekel (₪), ILS; ₪ 1 = 100 agorot
🛏️	**Hotels**	Porter ₪10–15; Chambermaid ₪10–15
🍴	**Restaurants**	Service charge included
🚗	**Taxis**	Round up

It is normal to see a service charge of around 15% added to most bills in Israel, be it for a meal in a **restaurant**, coffee in a **café** or for a stay in a **hotel**. This does not, however, eliminate the expectation of a tip. The custom of tipping is fairly common, but, of course, you should only leave some money if you feel the service has been good. In restaurants 10% should do the trick, although this is by no means standard – the amount left is very much up to the individual, while ₪ 10–15 is about right for porters or room staff; more if they're especially helpful.

Taxi drivers tend to expect a tip. Be sure to agree a price before taking a trip so it doesn't come as a shock at the end of your journey, and then round up or add more if you wish to do so, especially if your driver has helped with luggage. It is customary to tip **tour guides** and **drivers**. It depends on the service and the duration of the tour, but allow about ₪ 30–50 each per day or a proportion thereof, and more, arround ₪ 50–80, if you have a private guide.

When meeting people for the first time it is normal to shake hands. The important exception to this is if the other person is Orthodox or religious, in which case you should take your cue from their behaviour. Although Israelis drink very little, a gift of a bottle of wine will be appreciated if you are invited for dinner. If staying with someone a token gift from your home country, such as biscuits or old-fashioned sweets, will go down well.

Jordan

💰	**Currency**	Jordanian dinar, JOD, 1 dinar = 10 dirhams, 100 piastres or 1,000 fils
🛏	**Hotels**	Porter 1 dinar; Chambermaid 1 dinar
🍴	**Restaurants**	10%
🚕	**Taxis**	Round up

Jordan is a fascinating country with a friendly, largely Muslim, population that welcomes visitors; its tourism sector is well developed. One of the best ways of seeing Jordan's sights is to take a **tour**. You will find a tip for the tour guide and the driver is generally expected; allow around 3 dinar per person per day for the guide and a little less, around 2 dinar, for the driver. You might like to consider more for special interest guides. For example, on a diving trip you might consider upwards of 5 dinar to a maximum of around 10.

As regards **taxis**, if taking a short journey then the easiest option is to round up the amount shown on the meter to the nearest dinar, but for a longer journey agree a price to include a tip.

You will find that most **hotels** in Jordan add a service charge, but you might also like to offer around 1 dinar per bag to a porter, and about the same amount per day for the chambermaid. In **restaurants**, waiting staff generally expect a tip even though 10%

Top tip

Jordanians will greet with a handshake, although follow the lead of your host if of the opposite gender – for example: a male visitor meeting a female host should wait for her to offer her hand; a female visitor should wait for her male host to extend his hand.

is usually added to the bill for service. If the service has been good and your waiting staff friendly then you might like to offer around 2–3 dinars, or work on not more than 10% of the total bill. Although customary, tipping is always discretionary.

Jordanians are very hospitable and once you have established a rapport they will probably invite you to dine or take tea with their family. Gifts are welcome, but stick to pastries or confectionery, not alcohol which may not be welcomed.

Lebanon

🐚	**Currency**	Lebanese lira (LL), also known as the Lebanese pound (لل) (LBP)
🛏	**Hotels**	Porter لل3,000; Chambermaid لل3,000
🍴	**Restaurants**	10%
🚗	**Taxis**	Round up

Lebanon has long embraced the tipping culture with most service personnel expecting to receive something for their troubles. US dollars are also widely accepted here. In **hotels**, expect to tip around لل3,000 per bag for porters, with the same for chambermaids per day, and a smaller amount, around لل1,000, for doormen. In **restaurants**, add about 10% to the price of your meal for the waiting staff and give it direct. But whether you tip and how much you tip is entirely discretionary. Lebanese **taxis** are usually efficient and clean, and their drivers helpful. You can share a taxi with other passengers, known as servees, or book or hail a cab for personal use. In each case your taxi driver will not expect to be tipped, but rounding up to around 10% of the fare will usually be appreciated. For **tour guides and drivers**, consider giving around 5–10% of the fee. You will be expected to provide lunch for your guide and driver too, if engaging their services for a day's tour.

When accepting an invitation to dine with a local family, remember that Lebanon has a number of different ethnic groups, so unless you are sure of your host's religion it is perhaps safest to take pastries or a small gift of confectionery. Offer your gift with both hands. For business situations, your card should be offered with both hands, but there is no need to offer a gift. Always dress smartly and, if meeting your associate for the first time, expect a strong handshake and formality. Muslim men are unlikely to shake hands with women.

Oman

&#x2118;	**Currency**	Omani rial, OMR; 1 rial = 1,000 baisa
&#x1F3E8;	**Hotels**	Porter 1 rial; Chambermaid 1 rial
&#x1F37D;	**Restaurants**	Service charge included, otherwise 10–15%
&#x1F695;	**Taxis**	Round up

The Omani culture embraces rewarding those who have performed well, and it is customary to find a service charge of between 10% and 15% added to the bill in finer **restaurants** and almost all of the international-style **hotels**. On top of this, it is acceptable to tip a further 5% or so to the waiting staff if the service has been good. A tip should be given to your waiter personally and always in the local currency. If no service charge is included, tip around 10–15%. **Taxis** are best pre-arranged and a fare agreed. The fare will include a tip for the driver. If you wish to tip more it is acceptable to do so by rounding up or giving the change.

Omani people are hugely friendly and will shake your hand and impart pleasantries at both business and social occasions. The gesture is often complemented by placing a hand on the heart to convey sincerity. Business relationships are based on trust, and the giving of business gifts is unnecessary. If invited to a private home, consider it an honour. Hospitality is important in Oman and you will be assured a pleasant experience. Expect to be offered coffee and fruit (which you should not decline as this is seen as rude), followed by traditional dishes. Ideal gifts to take are traditional items from your home country, but avoid anything alcoholic or containing alcohol as this may not be welcomed.

Palestine

💰	**Currency**	New Israeli shekel (₪), ILS; ₪1 = 100 agorots
🛎	**Hotels**	Porter ₪20; Chambermaid ₪20
🍴	**Restaurants**	10–20%
🚗	**Taxis**	15–20%

Palestine has a tipping culture, although many of the larger hotels and restaurants will include a service charge, and it is considered discretionary if the customer wishes to leave more. Around 10% for the waiting staff in **restaurants** is about right, or as much as 20% if the service has been particularly attentive. In **hotels**, personnel you might like to tip include porters and chambermaids, for whom around ₪20 would be appropriate. If you use room service check that a service charge hasn't already been included. Tipping is not really expected in smaller establishments and those found in the more rural areas, but it would not cause offence and will probably be appreciated if you do tip.

Taxi drivers generally expect a tip of around 15–20% if using the meter, but if you've agreed a figure for a specified journey then the figure would include a gratuity. For **tour drivers** reckon on about 5% and tour guides around 10%, more if you feel the service has been especially good. When you are out and about you may be

Top tip

Drivers of shared taxis, known as *serveece* or *transeet*, don't generally expect to receive a tip, but be aware that they don't always carry change so you may be forced by circumstances to round up.

tempted to photograph locals in their traditional dress. Be aware that they will almost always expect you to give them ₪5–10 for the privilege of taking their photo.

Palestine has well-defined etiquette standards. If you are invited to share a drink or a meal with someone it would be considered offensive if you then tried to pay. Similarly, if invited to someone's home to dine you should not take food as a gift, as this would be considered an insult. Take a small gift for the host's children or a souvenir from your homeland instead. Avoid alcohol as a gift unless you know the person partakes. On arrival it is common practice to shake hands, but usually only between same sexes unless you're in an obviously modern household, in which case let your host or hostess initiate any physical contact. Dress modestly and do not show the soles of your feet, as this is considered offensive.

Qatar

🝔	**Currency**	Qatari riyal (QR), QAR; QR1 = 100 dirhams
🛏	**Hotels**	Porter QR5; Chambermaid QR5
🍴	**Restaurants**	Service charge included or 10%
🚗	**Taxis**	Round up

You will find that a service charge of around 10% is usually added to **hotel** and **restaurant** bills in Qatar, one of the richest countries off the Persian Gulf. It is not expected that you would wish to add anything extra to the bill. However, if there is no service charge applied then you might like to round up by up to 10%. If you plan to take a **taxi** during your stay you will find that the fare will almost certainly not include a tip, but then it is not something drivers expect. It is acceptable, however, and in many cases convenient, to simply round up the fare.

Prolonged greetings are the norm in Qatar, with polite enquiries and lengthy replies on both sides long before you can get down to business. Men should avoid enquiring after another man's wife unless he mentions her first. If you are invited to dine with a Qatari family, bring along a gift for your host's children.

Syria

☞	**Currency**	Syrian pound (S£), SYP; S£1 = 100 piastres
♨	**Hotels**	Porter S£55; Chambermaid S£55
⑪	**Restaurants**	5–10%
🚗	**Taxis**	Round up

While tipping is an accepted form of showing appreciation for good service, it is left entirely to the discretion of the individual. It is becoming commonplace to leave something for the **hotel** or **restaurant** staff, but as to the amount there are no hard and fast rules. A good guide is 5% to 10% of the bill. Restaurants do not, as a rule, add a service charge. **Taxi drivers** tend not to expect tips, but it is customary to offer something, so the most convenient way is to round up the fare by about 10%.

Hotel and airport porters often receive a few pounds for their assistance. Avoid offering a tip to someone who has simply done you a small favour and doesn't really work in the service industry. Syrians are friendly and dignified people and will offer help spontaneously if they think you need it. To offer money insults their honour.

Greetings are highly important in Syria, and you should not launch into a business matter or enquiry before you have exchanged the necessary salutations and enquired after the other person's health and family. Women should wait for a man to offer a handshake; if he holds his hand to his chest it means he is a practising Muslim, and cannot shake the hand of a woman who is not his wife or relation. If you are invited to a Syrian's house you should bring a small gift, such as a souvenir from your country or something for your host's children, as a sign of your appreciation. However, it is not customary for Syrian Arabs to express profuse gratitude over a gift, so do not be surprised if they offer rather muted thanks.

United Arab Emirates

💰	**Currency**	United Arab Emirates dirham (DH), AED; 1DH = 100 fils
🛎	**Hotels**	Porter 10DH; Chambermaid 10DH
🍴	**Restaurants**	10%
🚗	**Taxis**	Round up

Comprising Abu Dhabi, Ajman, Dubai, Fujairah, Ras al-Khaimah, Sharjah and Umm al-Quwain, the United Arab Emirates have a strong tradition of hospitality. You will always be treated politely and with respect, and of course you should reciprocate. Tipping is entirely discretionary and often a box is provided for you to place some coins in, which will be divided amongst staff. In some **hotels** and **restaurants** a service charge is included, particularly in the many finer venues. The levels of service are usually outstanding, and you may wish to leave a small cash tip of, say, 10DH to anyone who has been notably attentive and helpful to you. It is best to hand this additional tip to the waiter or waitress directly. If no service charge is included then you may like to tip 10–15DH or 10% in more upmarket establishments. It will always be appreciated, as service personnel often receive low wages. You should give around 10DH to porters per bag and the same for chambermaids per day, but

Top tip

The emirates all follow similar tipping practices. In Abu Dhabi, for example, taxi drivers and tour guides do not expect a tip, but will appreciate a little extra, while in restaurants 10% is considered adequate if service is excluded. If it is, then nothing further is expected.

other people like hairdressers and barbers tend to feel they charge a fair price and therefore do not expect anything further.

Taxi drivers and tour guides rarely have the look of anticipating a tip. It has not been traditionally appropriate to tip a taxi driver, but receiving one has become more commonplace as more people visit, bringing with them their own customs. The easiest way is to round up by about 10% of the value of the fare or tour price. It is customary to tip petrol attendants if they perform an extra service such as windscreen cleaning (5–10DH is ample).

The giving of gifts is widely practised in the United Arab Emirates, although never expected, and it is unnecessary for a business meeting. A gift to a host who has extended you an invitation to dine in his home, however, is always met with appreciation. Chocolate, fruits or an ornament from your home country are popular gifts, but always avoid alcohol of any description. Often the invitation to dine is regarded as a gift. If invited to dine in a person's private home then you will be expected to remove your shoes. You should always show respect and eat with your right hand. If you are giving a wrapped gift then offer it with your right hand.

Yemen

🪙	**Currency**	Yemeni rial (YR), YER
🛏	**Hotels**	Porter YR100–200; Chambermaid YR100–200
🍴	**Restaurants**	10%
🚗	**Taxis**	No tip

Tipping has not been commonly practised in Yemen, but these views are slowly changing as the country is opening itself up to the tourism industry.

As a general rule, tipping is expected (and appropriate) in places that cater primarily to the tourism industry, and it is not expected (although of course welcomed) in places that do not. Thus, for example, **tour guides** and **drivers** should both be tipped; the standard amount is YR2,000–3,000 per day and YR1,000–2,000 per day respectively. **Porters** who carry your luggage (at the hotel or the airport, for instance) should be tipped around YR200. Patrons at upscale **restaurants** at the more expensive hotels may leave a tip of around 10% of the total cost of a meal to the waiter. For children who provide small assistance such as a brief tour or giving directions, a gift of pens will go a long way. Tipping is not expected at restaurants that serve locals or with taxi drivers.

Formal suits are acceptable business attire in Yemen. Women should dress conservatively and make sure that they are covered from shoulders to ankles, preferably with a headscarf. It is not necessarily traditional to take a gift if invited to a Yemeni home for dinner, but something small and simple would be a good way of showing your appreciation. Avoid giving alcohol.

Asia and Australasia

Tipping in Asia and Australasia can be a tricky practice because while some countries expect it, others consider it an insult. You'll find countries like the Philippines, Kazakhstan, Kyrgyzstan, Indonesia and India tend to have a practice whereby most restaurants and some hotels include a service charge in the bill, while others like Australia tend to work on the basis that if someone wishes to tip it should be discretionary. In Japan and China it is an affront to offer a tip.

Armenia

🏦 **Currency**	Armenian dram (֏, AMD), AMD; AMD1 = 100 luma
🛏 **Hotels**	Porter AMD360; Chambermaid AMD360
🍴 **Restaurants**	10%
🚗 **Taxis**	10% or round up

Armenia has adopted a tipping culture, and waiters in restaurants and porters or doormen in hotels often expect a few coins in advance. The result is usually an attentive service. Many **restaurants** and **hotels** now include a 10% service fee, although it is not always stated on the menu or the bill itself. If unsure, ask whether it is included. You may wish to tip a waiter more for good service. Armenians tend to round up the cost of their meal to around 10% of its total, which is a good guide to follow.

Taxis usually represent good value by Western standards, although the price quoted is likely to include a hefty tip for the driver. It is best to ask and agree a price in advance. If a tip is included but your driver has shown you courtesy, and even helped with your luggage, you may like to round up or offer 10% for longer journeys, but it is entirely discretionary. You can book a cab in advance or at the airport.

Most business visitors will be taken to restaurants by their hosts for long meals and a succession of toasts. Armenians are extremely hospitable and visitors will often be invited into people's homes for coffee. If you are invited for a meal, whether to discuss business or for a social occasion, be punctual and smart, and expect to be plied with a lot of food. It is considered polite to at least try every dish.

A small gift such as chocolates or flowers (always an odd number) is appropriate for the hostess, who will have spent a great deal of time preparing the meal.

Australia

🪙	**Currency**	Australian dollar (A$), AUD; A$1 = 100 cents
🛎️	**Hotels**	Porter A$2–4; Chambermaid A$2
🍴	**Restaurants**	10%
🚗	**Taxis**	Round up

Service personnel in Australia are respected and generally paid a salary that ensures they don't have to rely on tips. Tipping has not been a way of life and some service workers have long regarded being offered a few coins as an insult. This view is changing, however, and Australians are beginning to see tipping as a gesture that shows the customer wishes to show gratitude, but it remains very much a personal choice. In the larger cities like Sydney, Melbourne and Perth, **hotels** and **restaurants**, plus a few nightclubs, now regard 10% as a fairly standard gratuity, but if a service charge has been built in then no tip should be left. Tips are usually offered to porters for helping with luggage, with A$2–4 per item about right. **Taxi drivers** generally include a service charge if quoting a fixed fare, but if not then the easiest thing is to round up or suggest the driver keep the change.

Australians are naturally friendly and may invite you to dine at their home if you get chatting. Dinner will often be a barbecue and there are no strict rules of etiquette. Everyone tends to address each other by their first names, even at the first meeting, and all will relax and have fun. Take a gift for your host or hostess. Good wine, chocolates or flowers are ideal for a dinner party, but barbecues are much less formal so take along wine or beer. One no-no is to talk business at a social occasion; that is left to office hours and usually by appointment. Business is a serious subject, but you'll find that offering a corporate-style gift is unnecessary.

Bangladesh

💰 **Currency**	Bangladeshi taka (Tk), BDT; Tk1 = 100 paisa	
🛏 **Hotels**	Porter Tk20; Chambermaid Tk20	
🍴 **Restaurants**	5%	
🚕 **Taxis**	Round up	

Bangladesh has a fascinating culture and vibrancy, with tourists swelling its numbers continuously. Its **hotels** and **restaurants**, especially those in Dhaka, its capital, have become accustomed to serving visitors and as such the practice of tipping has become customary. The standard is around 5% of the total bill, although considering the high poverty rate and low wages you might like to think about a little more, say around Tk20. Anything above this would appear over-generous and out of sync with the local culture. As a guide, allow Tk20 for hotel porters and about the same for chambermaids, while for **taxi** drivers the best solution if the journey has been pleasant and the driver helpful is to round up the fare.

Bangladeshis tend to shake hands in greeting, both in social and business environments, although women will probably only be greeted in this manner at the start of a business meeting. Business gifts are unnecessary; simply offer your business card, which should be done with your right hand. If invited to dine in a local family's home, then gifts of pastries or chocolates are the most appropriate. These should be given with both hands.

Borneo
(For Malaysia, see page 145)

🛥 **Currency**	Malaysian ringgit (RM), MYR; RM1 = 100 sen	
🛎 **Hotels**	Porter no tip; Chambermaid no tip	
🍴 **Restaurants**	No tip	
🚗 **Taxis**	No tip	

There is absolutely no expectation at all in Borneo to receive tips. The custom of tipping has no precedent in the Malaysian states of Sabah and Sarawak, nor in the Sultanate of Brunei. What holds for mainland Malaysia is even more the case on this laid-back island.

In **hotels**, leaving a small tip is fine, but not necessary. It is normal to leave a small amount for the housekeeping and bellboy of the hotel when checking out. Your guide will also happily accept a small gratuity if he has done a good job and you wish to show your appreciation. As to the amount, it is entirely up to you – the gesture is the important thing. It is common to offer tips to local **tour guides** and drivers, but rarely to **taxi** drivers. On the other hand, Borneo has its own set of rules when it comes to visitor etiquette, which ties in strongly with the cultural makeup of the place and enduring tribal life. You will be warmly received if you have the foresight to bring small gifts with you when visiting people in their homes, homestay tourism and longhouse visits.

The *tuai rumah* – longhouse chief – would much rather share some European chocolate (if it survives the heat!), among the people of his village, than divvy up a small sum of money, and they in turn will happily share rice wine with you.

China & Hong Kong

✉	**Currency**	China yuan renminbi (元), CNY; 元1 = 100 fen; Hong Kong dollar (HK$), HKD; HK$1 = 100 cents
🛎	**Hotels**	Porter 元15–20/HK$12; Chambermaid 元15/HK$10
🍴	**Restaurants**	Service charge included
🚕	**Taxis**	Round up or 10%

China's service personnel are not at all keen on the practice of tipping. Not only it is uncommon, officially not being a requirement of a customer, it is also considered rude. In the larger international **hotels** and top-end **restaurants**, a service charge of 10–15% is often included in the bill and no further gratuities are expected. If you have received exceptional service and wish to reward this with a tip, it is only in these establishments where it is likely to be understood. If you are unsure whether it would cause offence then check with the proprietor. Tipping airport porters is inappropriate, and often officially banned, but it is acceptable to offer 元15–20 or so per bag in a hotel. Tour companies in the international travel sector may expect you to show appreciation to your tour guide or driver in the form of gratuity of, say, 元60–100 per day; however, always abide by their rules as to the amount.

Hong Kong is a different matter altogether. A hustling, bustling cosmopolitan city, it has long had a penchant for tipping and this is done in most establishments. **Hotels** and **restaurants** usually include a service charge in their pricing structure as standard, but gratuities of around 10% on top are the norm. You'll find porters expect a dozen or so Hong Kong dollars per bag, probably more in the five-star glitzy hotels, and cloakroom attendants in the same hotels a few dollars. **Taxi drivers** will often, cheekily, round up the bill themselves when asking you to pay, so there's no need to offer any more unless you particularly wish to do so. If you are unsure if they've rounded up or not, just ask; if they haven't, you might like to do so yourself as this is discretionary.

Etiquette in China and Hong Kong differ too. Socially, the Chinese prefer to dine in a restaurant rather than in the home. If invited to someone's home, consider it a great honour and always take a gift of sweets, pastries or a fruit basket for the hostess. Business meetings in China are rarely done outside an office environment. You should never arrive late, which is considered insulting, and it is best not to take a gift until you are sure of your relationship. In Hong Kong, however, the giving and receiving of gifts is commonplace as part of business, but you should keep them business orientated. An invitation to a restaurant is considered a gift. In fact, dining in restaurants forms a key part of doing business in Hong Kong. If invited to someone's home, do take a gift for the hostess – chocolate or pastries would be appropriate.

Georgia

⌕	**Currency**	Georgian lari (GEL), GEL; GEL1 = 100 tetri
🏨	**Hotels**	Porter GEL2; Chambermaid GEL2
🍴	**Restaurants**	10%
🚗	**Taxis**	Round up

Georgia's service personnel are generally friendly and, where once tipping was strictly discouraged, it is becoming more and more a part of everyday life in hotels and restaurants. As a result, waiters now have good reason to serve you well and are appreciative of any gratuity you might like to offer. Of course, bad service still doesn't warrant a tip. In the main, it is appropriate to round up the bill if you are dining in a **restaurant** or café rather than to add a percentage to the amount. It's a similar case if you are taking a **taxi** or using the services of a **guide**. In markets, however, it is considered good form to haggle for a bargain, and you can actually get the price down by as much as 30%. Allow around GEL2 for porters and chambermaids in **hotels**. Georgian culture is very much about getting together, whether it be with family, friends or business associates. As such, events and even business meetings tend to be relaxed. If visiting someone at home, you will find the welcome to be warm and genuine. Gifts of chocolates for the host or a small gift for the family's children will always be gratefully received. Business gifts are unnecessary; just offer your card after the handshakes and introductions initiated by your host are concluded.

India

🖎	**Currency**	Indian rupee (₹), INR; ₹1 = 100 paise
🛏	**Hotels**	Porter ₹30; Chambermaid ₹30
🍴	**Restaurants**	Service charge included
🚗	**Taxis**	Round up or 10%

A 10% service charge and varying degrees of luxury tax are generally included in your bill when staying in a **hotel** or dining in a **restaurant**, and any gratuities on top of this are entirely discretionary. Around 10% or ₹60 is generally acceptable for waiting staff, even though it seems to be a rather small sum. Porters and chambermaids generally receive about ₹30. Carry some loose change to tip anyone who helps you when you are out and about, or provides a type of service. The latter might include people who will happily pose for photographs, although note that it can be problematic photographing women, depending on the region, and it might be considered impolite to do so. Do remember that there are two forms of tipping: the traditional version, and *baksheesh* when you tip in advance to ensure good service.

If you are taking a **taxi** or a three-wheeler it is generally best to round up the fare to the nearest ₹10. If you have agreed a price in advance then your fare will, in all likelihood, include a gratuity for the driver. If you are taking a group guided tour then consider about ₹100 per day for the **guide**, but double if you are taking a private tour.

Take a small gift when dining with someone in their home. Avoid alcohol unless you know their religion, and do not take white flowers as these are associated with funerals. Do not wrap gifts in white or black, which are considered unlucky colours. You may be required to tip their domestic staff if you are staying overnight – it's worth asking your host and, if it is expected, check how much to offer.

Indonesia

&#x1F4B0;	**Currency**	Indonesia rupiah (Rp), IDR
&#x1F3E8;	**Hotels**	Porter Rp2,000–5,000; Chambermaid Rp1,000
&#x1F37D;	**Restaurants**	Service charge included
&#x1F697;	**Taxis**	Round up or Rp2,000

You are almost guaranteed good service wherever you go in Indonesia. In **hotels** and **restaurants**, especially the Westernised ones, you might see a service charge of 10% added to the menu price; if you don't then you can round up or add a little extra if you wish, but tipping is not generally a way of life in hotels and restaurants here. **Airport porters** tend to expect about Rp5,000 per bag, and hotel porters around Rp2,000. If you are visiting a **temple** or an **art museum** then a donation is the normal custom, with no further tip to staff necessary. Reckon on about Rp2,000 tip for **taxi drivers**, but less if the service hasn't been great. Rounding up works too.

The giving of gifts in Indonesia can be a minefield. The country is made up of thousands of islands that are home to 300 or so ethnic groups, including Sundanese, Javanese and Malay. The choice of gift and the way it is given, both socially and in business, can vary enormously between the ethnic groups. Because Indonesians do not like uncomfortable situations, if you need help as to what gift is most suitable, your hosts or their associates are usually happy to discreetly advise. Indonesians, in general, appreciate anything that is of foreign origin, so a gift from your homeland is a safe bet. It is good practice to arrive for any occasion promptly, although arriving late is unlikely to offend as Indonesians have a fairly flexibly approach to timekeeping. On meeting, shake hands, although never use your left hand as this is insulting, and present a name or business card.

Japan

✍	**Currency**	Japanese yen (¥), JPY; ¥1 = 100 sen
☰	**Hotels**	Porter no tip; Chambermaid no tip
❙❙	**Restaurants**	Service charge included
▄	**Taxis**	No tip necessary

It is not the custom to tip in Japan. In fact, if you leave a few coins or notes on a restaurant table after your meal your waiter or waitress is just as likely to think you have forgotten to take your change and run after you to return it. If you offer a tip directly it will almost certainly be refused with a polite 'no thank you', as it is insulting and unacceptable to demean someone in such a way. In some of the larger international **hotels** and **restaurants** you may find a 10–15% service charge has been added to your bill, which is becoming more and more customary, but certainly no further gratuity is expected. Similarly, bar staff, reception staff and hotel porters do not expect a tip, although some hotels can provide you with a small envelope should you wish to reward exceptional service discreetly – for instance, if you had to call upon a hotel staff member in the event of a problem and they spent some time helping you.

Elsewhere, **airport** and **railway porters** work to a pre-defined tariff, which you agree to if you engage their services. Hairdressers, barbers, guides and taxi drivers do not expect gratuities of any kind.

Top tip

You would not normally tip staff in a *ryokan* (a Japanese-style inn), but the rare exception is an exclusive *ryokan*, where you offer a gratuity to the head member of staff.

Social and business etiquette is valued and expected in Japan. If invited to dine with a family then always take a gift. A beautifully wrapped food basket is ideal. Even if you have spent a lot of money on the gift, it is polite to apologise for its inadequacy. A gadget would make a good business gift, but be sure you have established a relationship and achieved mutual respect first before giving it. If wrapping a gift, avoid the colours white and black as they relate to bereavement.

Kazakhstan

🖎	**Currency**	Kazakh tenge (T), KZT; T1 = 100 tiyin
🏨	**Hotels**	Porter T100–200; Chambermaid T150
🍴	**Restaurants**	Service charge included
🚗	**Taxis**	Round up

Offering gratuities in Kazakhstan is all rather organised, which is often a blessing for tourists unsure of what is acceptable and what is not. **Hotels** and **restaurants** apply a 10% service charge to the price you pay for a meal, and no further tip is necessary or expected. Tipping is, however, becoming more common in top-range hotels, including for restaurant service. Porters should be tipped where this

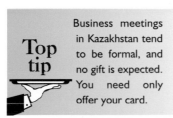

Top tip

Business meetings in Kazakhstan tend to be formal, and no gift is expected. You need only offer your card.

service is provided: at the time of writing T200 was about the going rate. **Taxi** fares are fixed and it is not necessary to offer anything more than the stated amount. If you are taking a **tour**, then a tip or a small gift for your tour guide and driver would be appreciated, although is not generally expected.

Consider it an honour to be invited to dine in a Kazakh's home, and expect a large gathering of family members. You should take a gift; a souvenir from your home country works well. Otherwise, flowers or chocolates are always acceptable.

Kyrgyzstan

🛢	**Currency**	Kyrgyz som, KGS; 1som = 100 tiyins
🛏	**Hotels**	Porter 50som; Chambermaid 50som
🍴	**Restaurants**	Service charge included or 10%
🚗	**Taxis**	Round up

It is becoming more common to tip in Kyrgyzstan. Some upmarket **hotels** and **restaurants** will add a service charge of as much as 15% to the bill, so do check before deciding what amount to add for exceptional service. Adding a further 10% or so may sometimes be expected in places frequented by tourists. **Taxi** drivers will take you anywhere you ask; negotiate the fare first of all and round up.

The Kyrgyzstan people are welcoming of visitors and often extend invitations to dine in a restaurant or in their own home. Always take a small but not extravagant gift for the host. Something from your own country would be welcome, or opt for fruit or pastries. Drinks need not be drained – to do so invites a refill. Shoes should always be removed when entering a house or yurt.

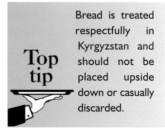

Top tip

Bread is treated respectfully in Kyrgyzstan and should not be placed upside down or casually discarded.

Malaysia

(For Borneo, see page 135)

✆	**Currency**	Malaysian ringgit (RM), MYR; RM1 = 100 sen
🛏	**Hotels**	Porter no tip; Chambermaid no tip
🍴	**Restaurants**	Service charge included
🚕	**Taxis**	Round up

Malaysia is not traditionally a tipping society, but Western influences have changed things a little, especially in the larger cities and spots frequented by tourists. Tip with care, however, as it is often still considered rude. **Hotels** increasingly add a 10% service charge to the cost of a room, and top-end **restaurants** 10–15% to their menu or bill prices. Yet not all do, so if you wish to tip you can round up or add the equivalent for the staff. Hotel **porters**, particularly those in luxury or five-star establishments, are beginning to accept the notion of tipping, and you may like to offer something. Around RM5 per bag would be appropriate.

Agree **taxi** fares in advance in an unmetered cab, but expect a bit of hard bargaining. Alternatively, you could make sure the meter is on, and round up to the nearest ringgit at the end of the journey. It is becoming more common to tip **tour guides**; a suitable rate would be about 10% of the price you paid for the tour.

Business etiquette in Malaysia can seem a little complicated at first. Always shake hands or pass your business card with your right hand, never your left, and do not point or gesture with your foot. The giving of gifts is also complex. In business, wait for the lead from your associate and then reciprocate. Socially, take a food hamper or a gift from your own country for your hosts when dining in their home: avoid giving alcohol unless you know your hosts' ethnic group.

Maldives

🪙 **Currency**	Maldives rufiyaa (Rf), MVR; Rf1 = 100 laari. US dollars (US$) predominantly used in resorts	
🛏 **Hotels**	Porter US$5; Chambermaid US$5	
🍴 **Restaurants**	10%	
🚕 **Taxis**	Round up	

Tipping is officially discouraged in the Maldives, but neither guests nor servers take any notice of that. However, the boatmen (unless you are on a **liveaboard safari boat**, in which case the crew will expect about US$5 a day) and **taxi drivers** won't expect a tip. Some **hotels** do not add a service charge to the room-only bill, in which case you should reward your room boy from around US$5 a day depending on the room rate, up to US$20 per day for a suite for two. Tip the room service waiter about 5% of the bill in cash. Porters who bring your luggage to the room should be tipped about US$5 on arrival and departure. Spa staff should be tipped and the spa receptionist will give guidelines. **Restaurants** and bars add a service charge, and a cash tip of about 5% in the bar each time you sign a bill is a good gesture that will bring results. At the end of your stay the waiter who has served you regularly should be tipped about US$5 per day of your stay, with an extra US$20 each for the captain/supervisor and wine waiter if they have been helpful. When dining in an à la carte restaurant (as opposed to a package-deal buffet) tip 5% of the bill in cash if a service charge of 10% or more shows on the bill. Tipping of **dive school** or watersports centre staff can work wonders. With most of the frontline staff of all resorts being foreigners, they will expect to be rewarded for any service and Maldivians (who usually serve as waiters) expect the same.

Top tip

Always tip in US dollars, as it is an official currency in the Maldives. There is no need to change foreign currency into local Maldivian rufiyaas.

Gifts are not expected but widely given in the Maldives, especially from guests when dining in someone's home. By far the best gift is something from your own country, such as a small item of craftwork.

Greet your host with a handshake, both in business and socially, and be prepared to remove your shoes when entering someone's home. A discreet glance at your host's feet will reveal whether this will be expected of you.

Mongolia

🐚	**Currency**	Currency Mongolian tögrög (₮), MNT; ₮1 = 100 möngö
🛏	**Hotels**	Porter no tip; Chambermaid no tip
🍴	**Restaurants**	10%
🚗	**Taxis**	Round up

Located between Russia and China, Mongolia is used to receiving visitors. **Hotels** and **restaurants** that cater for tourists do not generally include a service charge in their bill, and it is left to the individual to decide when and how much to reward for good service. The unwritten industry standard of 10% is about right. You would not be expected to tip bellboys or other service personnel such as chambermaids, and similarly staff in cafés and bars and **taxi drivers** do not expect to receive any money other than the amount tendered. If you are taking a **tour** of two or three weeks' duration in Mongolia it is customary to tip generously. As a guide, allow around the equivalent of ₮60 for the cook per group, ₮75 per group for other tour staff and ₮110 per group for the driver.

Mongolians are hospitable people. Should you be invited to dine, give a gift on departure, not on arrival, with something from your home country being suitable. Take at least a bite or sip of any delicacies offered and receive food (or gifts) with the right hand supported at the wrist or elbow by the left hand.

Nepal

☞ **Currency**	Nepalese rupee (Rs), NPR; Rs1 = 100 paisa
♨ **Hotels**	Porter no tip; Chambermaid no tip
ⲓⲓ **Restaurants**	Service charge included or 10%
🚗 **Taxis**	Round up

Service workers' views in Nepal appear to lie somewhere between not expecting a form of gratuity out of politeness and pride, and the need for extra money to boost often low wages. For the visitor it is a bit of a dilemma. **Restaurants** generally add 10% to their bills, which is usually distributed amongst staff, so no further tipping is necessary. For the establishments that don't include a service charge then a 10% gratuity should do the trick, or you could simply round up the bill. **Hotels** may add 10% on top of the standard room rate, plus a further 13% for VAT, but remember that out of peak season you may be able to negotiate a discount. A service charge is generally customary in tourist areas. It is not generally accepted that you will tip service personnel such as porters or hotel room staff, indeed the unwritten rule is no tip. However, since wages are often low you might like to offer something and around Rs30 to each is neither insulting nor too generous.

Equally customary is to tip the hard-worked **guides**, sherpas and porters on the treks into the mountains for which many, if not most, visitors come to Nepal. It is usual for the leader of the trek, the person who represents the company you have booked with, to collect whatever everyone wishes to give at the end and distribute it fairly amongst the crew. The leader will often recommend an appropriate amount, which is likely to be in the region of US$3 per person per day in local currency. At this rate with, say, eight trekkers on a 10-day trip, the resulting amount of US$240 equalling around

Rs18,000 will be a handsome reward for the team. A tip is regarded as a gesture to show you have enjoyed your experience, and is received with a sense of pride for a job done well. Porters carry huge amounts of trekkers' equipment. If you have enjoyed your trek, then to not tip is really somewhat unkind – tip as much as you can. As well as making a financial contribution to the trekking crew, an idea is to consider throwing in clothing and equipment that you don't want to take home with you. This is more than a tip: that equipment may not even be available to buy in Nepal, so your cast-offs may be considered a real treasure by a porter.

For **taxis**, it is often easier to round up to the nearest Rs100, but if your taxi doesn't have a meter, or one that works, negotiate a fee before you start your journey, and include any gratuity.

If invited to dine with a Nepalese family, use your judgment of the situation to decide whether to bring a gift or whether to try to repay their generosity in some other way – a modern family in Kathmandu is quite different from a hut in the foothills of Annapurna. In the

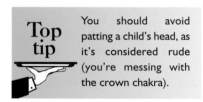

Top tip

You should avoid patting a child's head, as it's considered rude (you're messing with the crown chakra).

hills, you may want to give a gift if someone does you a favour such as allowing you to stay on their sleeping loft. You should avoid giving meat or meat by-products such as leather as a gift. In Nepal, gift-giving or receiving is always done with the right hand; the left hand is considered 'polluted'.

New Zealand

🪙	**Currency**	New Zealand dollar (NZ$), NZD; NZ$1 = 100 cents
🛏	**Hotels**	Porter no tip; Chambermaid no tip
🍴	**Restaurants**	10%
🚕	**Taxis**	Round up or 10%

Staying in lovely hotels, dining out in restaurants or heading out in your campervan on a tour of the countryside is all part of the lifestyle in New Zealand, for locals as well as visitors. Everyone is expected to pay the going rate, and is generally happy to do so. No further gratuities are expected by those providing the service – tipping is quite simply not a way of life. It is looked upon as an unnecessary thing to do, and by many it is even considered a bit of an insult. **Hotels** and **restaurants** do not add a service charge to their bills, the only exception being that some have started to add a percentage on bank holidays to cover any additional costs in engaging staff. Some restaurants and cafés may have a bowl to place loose change in.

Having said all that, many of the people employed in the service industry are students who probably receive a low wage. If you receive exceptionally good service (perhaps someone has been especially kind or helped you with a problem) then you might like to give them something in the region of NZ$8–10 as a show of

Top tip

Credit cards, which usually have a minimum spend, are widely accepted, as is cash. Should you wish to tip using your credit card make this clear, as even in restaurants you are unlikely to be offered the opportunity.

gratitude. It is understood that it has been given on merit and not because a customer feels an obligation. Rounding up the bill in a hotel or restaurant or leaving some change on the table is probably the most discreet, but you may find the waiter or waitress calls you back to return the money. It's more likely that they will think you've made a mistake rather than intentionally leaving a tip.

When you are on a tour or taking a taxi, it's generally a good policy to offer a gratuity to your **guide** or **driver**, even though they may not be expecting anything of you. If you round up to about the 10% mark in the case of a taxi, and about the same percentage to a guide, then you will be on the right track. Don't be offended if it is politely handed back to you, however. Tipping is becoming more widespread but many New Zealanders still feel a little uncomfortable with the custom.

The giving of gifts and social and business etiquette can be confusing because New Zealand is very much a multicultural country. Kiwi Pakeha (the Maori term for white Europeans) and Maori cultures can differ significantly. Finding out in advance about the person or people you are meeting in a business or social situation often proves a wise move. Whereas an appointment and handshakes generally do the trick in most situations, if you have dealings with tribal groups be prepared for more defined processes of welcoming, such as the Hongi where noses are pressed in greeting, and dining. In general, if you take gifts choose flowers or chocolate, and keep them simple.

Philippines

☞ **Currency**	Philippine peso (P), PHP; P1 = 100 centavos	
🛎 **Hotels**	Porter P100; Chambermaid P80	
🍴 **Restaurants**	Service charge included	
🚗 **Taxis**	Round up	

Until really quite recently it wasn't the custom to tip in the Philippines; however, thinking has changed significantly as Westerners travel to these idyllic islands, bringing with them their own values, and Filipinos themselves travel to other shores. Now it is quite common to see a service charge of around 10% automatically added to **hotel** and **restaurant** prices, especially the major international establishments. On top of this, service personnel have begun to expect a further gratuity.

Of course, whether to tip and by how much depends very much on the individual. There is no standard percentage, but if in doubt the old favourite of 10% is usually about right. If you find there's no service charge added then you might like to offer a little more. It really is discretionary. Bellboys usually expect their service to be rewarded, but by how much is left to you. About P50–100 per bag would be about right.

Taxis are a different matter. The drivers in Manila have a bit of a reputation for adding a cut for themselves when quoting a fare. Some may not put on the meter so it's difficult to argue at the end of your journey. It is far better to prearrange a taxi or, at least, agree a price. If the latter, you can still be sure there's a tip in there somewhere, so don't worry about tipping further.

If you are invited to a Filipino's home, always dress smartly, arrive punctually and take a gift for the host's wife. Confectionery is ideal. It

Top tip

Not all taxi drivers in the Philippines share a reputation for unscrupulousness with their Manila brethren. In Davao, a vibrant, cosmopolitan city on the island of Mindanao in the south of the country, and a favourite haunt of travellers, your taxi driver will almost certainly put on the meter and give you the exact change because you can report them for misconduct and will be given a telephone number to call should you wish to do so. The Davao drivers are permitted to accept tips, however, so if yours has been especially helpful (by carrying luggage, for instance) then you might like to round up the fare or offer about 10% extra.

is also considered polite to send a thank you note. In business, you can expect to be greeted with a handshake. Offer your card with both hands and always accept any hospitality given. To refuse is impolite.

Singapore

℘	**Currency**	Singapore dollar (S$), SGD; S$1 = 100 cents
▥	**Hotels**	Porter S$1–2; Chambermaid S$1–2
ⵌ	**Restaurants**	Service charge included
🚗	**Taxis**	Round up

Tipping in Singapore is simply not the done thing, with the exceptions being small gratuities to **porters**, to whom you would offer S$1–2 per bag, and **chambermaids**. In fact, the government actively discourages anyone from offering or leaving gratuities of any amount over and above the 10% service charge that is added to bills, plus a 4% government tax in most **hotels** and **restaurants**. **Taxi drivers** do not expect tips, but it is common to round up a fare to the nearest Singaporean dollar.

The giving of gifts is generally only done between friends or if you are invited to someone's home. If the latter, it is considered good manners to arrive punctually and take a small gift for the host or his wife. A fruit basket or confectionery are usually the safest gift options because not only are there several different ethnic groups with their own beliefs in Singapore, there are also associations attributed to certain items. For example, certain flowers and colours are associated with death. In any other situation, at the start of a business arrangement for instance, it is inappropriate to give a gift of any sort until you have formed a strong relationship of mutual respect. Do, however, present your business card and accept your associate's card gratefully.

South Korea

🕭	**Currency**	South Korean won (₩), KRW; ₩1 = 100 jeon
🏨	**Hotels**	Porter ₩1,000; Chambermaid ₩1,000
🍴	**Restaurants**	10%
🚗	**Taxis**	No tip

Tipping is not part of South Korean culture, although international **hotels** now add a 10% service charge with no further tips necessary. Similarly, sleek **restaurants** normally include a 10% service charge on the bill, but staff are allowed to accept tips. However, there's no need to tip at a South Korean barbecue joint. Porters in tourist and business hotels usually expect to get ₩500–1,000 per bag. When the 'porter service' is used at airports there's a fixed charge for each cart (₩3,000 at the time of writing), and no further tip is required. **Taxi drivers** don't expect tips, but if you're feeling generous you could offer to let them keep the change.

Exchanging gifts is normal in business circles. Corporate gifts complete with logos are generally acceptable.

Upon accepting a social invitation to a South Korean's home, take fruit or good-quality chocolates. It is inconsiderate to present an expensive gift if you know the recipient cannot afford to reciprocate at the same level. Take care in gift wrapping to follow local culture. Most Koreans use pattered paper with a white background or paper with some kind of abstract design. Avoid wrapping your gift in black or red paper. Avoid giving gifts in multiples of four. Seven of an item is considered lucky. When giving or receiving a gift, use both hands. Gifts are not opened when received. It is customary for guests to meet elsewhere first and travel together. Remove your shoes before entering someone's home.

Sri Lanka

🐚	**Currency**	Sri Lanka rupee, LKR; Rs1 = 100 cents
🛏	**Hotels**	Porter Rs500, Chambermaid Rs500
🍴	**Restaurants**	10% Service charge included, plus 5% for staff
🚗	**Taxis**	5% or Rs500 per day

A 10% service charge is generally added to hotel and **restaurant** bills, which is shared around the basic staff according to the establishment's formula, with a hefty amount for the hotel or restaurant manager. If you want to make sure the server gets the tip, give 5% (of the actual bill) in cash direct. Note that after the 10% service charge has been added to the bill, up to a further 17% is added for various taxes, so do not calculate the 5% on the final total but just give half the service charge in cash. Some restaurant bills are presented as 'Nett' which means that the service charge is included, and possibly the taxes too. Where that happens calculate 5% of the total bill and slip that to the server in cash. In a bar, if a bill is presented, add 5%. If no bill is given, round up to the nearest Rs100. In a local **café**, leaving loose change for the meal is customary.

For the **hotel** doorman tip Rs100 every day that he helps; for the porter tip Rs100 for every bag he carries into and out of the hotel. For the room boy (or chambermaid), reckon on Rs100 to Rs500 a day, per room, depending in the star grade of the hotel. Give the room service waiter Rs100 cash, or more if you have made an expensive order. Some five-star hotels have butlers who should be rewarded with Rs500 a day, depending on how helpful they are.

Tipping **three-wheeler drivers** is based on what price you negotiate for a journey before travelling; the driver will probably build in a tip in the price he quotes. Otherwise add Rs10 to Rs20, or

Top tip

Look out for the airport banks as you arrive. They give much better exchange rates than at hotels. Ask for small denomination notes so you have rupees immediately available for tipping *en route* to your hotel for the taxi driver and porters.

round up the price to the nearest Rs100. Drivers of hotel cars and metered **taxis** could be tipped 10% of the agreed charge, or Rs500 per day for a full day's hire, multiplied by the number of days of hire, if it's an island tour. If your group is more than two people, make that Rs500 per day per couple.

If you have any incoming deliveries (such as a meal or a courier package), or if a boy from a supermarket or other shop helps load your purchases into your vehicle, Rs100 is fine as a tip. Do not get yourself encumbered with a freelance guide as they will be seeking a commission from whatever you spend, as well as a tip. However, authorised **guides** at cultural sites will expect a tip and will inform you of the rate. Airport porters on departure (and arrival) have the per piece price stencilled on their waistcoats, so add Rs100 to the total. Snake charmers or drummers will demand Rs1,000 if you photograph them, so make sure you negotiate first. Try to ignore beggars, but if your conscience won't allow that, resist being too generous and give Rs20. Tip only in Sri Lankan rupees.

The standard greeting in Sri Lanka is *ayubown* ('may you have a long life'), which you should say while keeping your own hands, palms together, at chest height. If someone greets you this way, respond in kind. Handshaking is also generally acceptable. If invited to dinner in a Sri Lankan home. Avoid giving flowers as a gift.

Taiwan

🪙	**Currency**	New Taiwan dollar (NT$), TWD; NT$1
🛏	**Hotels**	Porter no tip; Chambermaid no tip
🍴	**Restaurants**	Service charge included
🚗	**Taxis**	Round up

Other than for airport porters, to whom about NT$50–100 per bag should be offered, tipping is simply not done in Taiwan. Although as more Western-style eating chains open, the thinking is gradually changing. **Hotels**, **restaurants** and other eateries prefer to add a service charge and, although they accept that their staff may be rewarded for good service and will turn a blind eye, no further gratuity is really necessary. **Taxi drivers**, similarly, do not expect you to offer a tip. If they have been enormously helpful to you and you wish to show appreciation, however, providing you offer a small amount diplomatically so as not to offend, then it will probably be greeted with a smile. Rounding up to the nearest NT$50 is appreciated but not at all expected.

Shaking hands is common when conducting business in Taiwan, but kissing women on the cheek is taboo. When dining out, it is good policy to offer to pay, but don't be surprised if the offer is politely declined. It is considered polite to top up your companions' glasses first when drinking.

Do take a gift if invited to a Taiwanese person's home. Fruit is a good choice, but cheaper varieties like bananas and guava should be avoided. If you decide to bring alcohol, go for a bottle of good whisky or red wine. The one no-no is offering your host or hostess a clock, as this implies that you want the recipient to die! Don't be alarmed if your host initially refuses your gift – this is a sign of politeness. Offer it again, and they will eventually accept.

Thailand

🖉	**Currency**	Thailand baht (฿), THB; ฿1 = 100 satangs
🛏	**Hotels**	Porter ฿20–50; Chambermaid ฿20
🍴	**Restaurants**	Service charge 10%, otherwise tip 10%
🚗	**Taxis**	Round up

Confusion reigns with the small change of Thai coins. Only the newer coins of one, two, five and ten baht have numerals understandable by most visitors.

There's no tradition of tipping in Thailand, but it's spreading from the tourist influx. The key figure is the 10% service charge on upmarket **hotels** and **restaurants**, but in Bangkok anything goes. That also applies to tipping. Some staff expect a gratuity; others don't. The more an establishment caters for foreigners, the greater likelihood that tips become part of staff income. It is customary to tip chambermaids, but they'll never remind you with an outstretched hand when you depart. Hotel porters expect about ฿30–50. Off the main tourist trails, hotels don't include a service charge, but staff members tend to appreciate something like ฿10–20 for carrying bags to your room. Tipping in Thailand is never an obligation. It's a gift you give to someone who deserves it. If a restaurant doesn't include a service charge in the bill, waiters will appreciate a 10% tip.

On the transport front, metered **taxis** are widely available in Bangkok, but not so much elsewhere. Fares are reasonable and tipping unnecessary, though people usually round up the fare. If your cab has no meter, always agree a price before starting. Hotel taxis operate with fixed rates which are usually more expensive, though the drivers are more likely to speak some English.

In Thailand the traditional form of greeting is the *wai*, which involves raising both hands, palms together with fingers pointing

Top tip

Tuk-tuks (also known as *samlors*) are motorised three-wheeler taxis that sound like mobile chainsaws at full speed. They are cheap – roughly half the price of regular taxis – and amusing to ride once or twice for short distances as a tourist experience. Pedal *samlors* (bicycle rickshaws) are available in many tourist places, and are a tranquil way of sightseeing. Fix the price first, and then no tipping will be necessary.

upwards, and raised to a point somewhere between the chest and the forehead. You show respect and thanks by the height at which you hold your hands and how low you bow your head. The strong sense of hierarchy means that you should wait for your host or hostess to introduce you to other guests, so that they know how to perform the *wai* towards you. Punctuality and courtesy are highly prized when conducting business. You should dress conservatively and try to give your business card to the most senior person first.

You are not required to bring a gift if invited to dine in a Thai home, but it will be gratefully received if you do. Nicely presented chocolates, fruit or flowers would be just right, although you should avoid using red wrapping paper. Traditionally Thais do not open gifts when they are given.

Vietnam

🍲	**Currency**	Vietnam dong (đ), VND; đ1 = 10 hào
🛏	**Hotels**	Porter đ1,000; Chambermaid no tip
🍴	**Restaurants**	10% service charge often included, otherwise 10%
🚗	**Taxis**	Round up

Vietnamese people often live on small wages, so providing a good service that may be rewarded with a tip has become accepted, even though traditionally it has not been a way of life. As more and more international hotel chains and upmarket restaurants that attract visitors have opened, and their waiting staff are experiencing a culture of tipping, then so employees of smaller restaurants and 'dust cafés' have come to see the benefits of earning a little extra. In reality, a 10% tip based on the price of a meal is a small amount to the average Western traveller, which should be given directly to the individual in local cash. Be aware that many of the **hotels** and **restaurants** run by the government for tourists automatically add a 10% service charge, and it will be left to your discretion if you wish to leave more. In hotels, the service charge covers the services of chambermaids, but not porters, to whom you may like to offer change in local currency. Be careful not to offend and always voice your thanks. **Taxi drivers**, similarly, do not expect to receive a tip, although it is the norm to round up the fare. One of the best ways to see Vietnam is to take a **tour** of several days' duration, in which case reckon on around US$1 per day for the driver-cum-guide. If you are taking a day tour then there's no need to tip. The driver-guide would not expect it.

In social situations you should greet the oldest person present first. Punctuality is considered very important in business. At meetings, handshakes are only usually exchanged between members of the same sex. A token gift, such as an item showing your company's logo, will be accepted.

On entering a Vietnamese person's home you should remove your shoes and, by way of greeting, press your hands together and bow slightly. A gift such as fruit, sweets or incense, wrapped in bright paper, is ideal if you are invited for dinner in a Vietnamese home.

Central and South America

Tipping practices in Central and South America can vary significantly between countries, and even regions within each country. Most work on about 10–15% in hotels and restaurants, such as in Brazil and Belize, while in some the figure is a little less. You will often see a service charge added to or included in the bill.

Argentina

🪙	**Currency**	Argentinean peso ($), ARS; 1 peso = 100 centavos
🛏	**Hotels**	Porter 3 pesos; Chambermaid 3 pesos
🍴	**Restaurants**	10–15%
🚗	**Taxis**	Round up

Tipping in Argentina has become a way of life, and **hotels** and **restaurants** in tourist areas have even become a little more regulated when it comes to what has traditionally been a thorny issue. It is now becoming more accepted to tip for good service at around 10% of the bill value, irrespective of whether a service charge is included. If you see the fixed price *cubierto*, usually at the start of your bill, this is a charge for the table setting and bread, and not the tip for the waiting staff.

Elsewhere, **hotel and airport porters** tend to expect around 2–3 pesos per bag, with doormen a little more, and chambermaids around 4–5 pesos per day. It is not necessary to tip in bars, but you may like to leave loose change if you have been served at your table. If travelling by **taxi**, prearrange a price – this will probably include a gratuity for the driver. Alternatively, it is fine to round up the fare.

Initial greetings are usually fairly formal, with handshakes being the norm. If you are there on business, it is important to dress well for meetings and it is a good idea to have one side of your business card translated into Spanish. Only give a gift in a business situation once your relationship has been established. A bottle of whisky or brandy is a good idea, as tax on such items is high. Bottles of spirits also go down a treat as a gift for the host or hostess if you are invited to dine in an Argentinean home. Be sure to arrive about half an hour after the appointed time; arriving absolutely punctually is not expected.

Belize

🐚	**Currency**	Belizean dollar (BZ$), BZD; BZ$1 = 100 cents
🛏	**Hotels**	Porter no tip; Chambermaid no tip
🍴	**Restaurants**	10–15%
🚗	**Taxis**	Round up

Belize's **hotels** and **resorts**, many of which are upmarket, tend to add a 10% service charge automatically to guests' bills. This charge is divided amongst porters, chambermaids and other service personnel, and you would not be expected to leave any further gratuity. **Restaurants** are different. They do not generally add a service charge to a bill and, in fact, actively encourage diners to tip waiters and waitresses to boost their salaries. The 'going rate' for tips is between 10% and 15% of the bill – the more exclusive and expensive the restaurant, the higher the percentage.

In the case of taxis, you will find **taxi drivers** do not generally expect tips for getting you to your destination, but if they are especially helpful or assist you with your bags rounding up the bill to at least 10% would always be met with appreciation. If you take a short tour during your stay then consider a tip of a few dollars for the **guide**. For a special interest tour or one of several days duration you might like to work on 10–15% of the total price you paid for the tour if you are happy with the service you received.

Belizeans are friendly people and usually more than happy to pose so you can take their photograph. Do give them a few dollars as a thank you. If you make a friend during your stay you are very likely to be invited to his or her home to dine, in which case take a small gift of something edible, like a fruit basket or pastries for the hostess.

Bolivia

🪙	**Currency**	Bolivian boliviano (Bs), BOB; 1Bs = 100 centavos
🛏	**Hotels**	Porter 7Bs; Chambermaid 7Bs
🍴	**Restaurants**	10–15%
🚗	**Taxis**	Round up or 10%

Tipping is a way of life in Bolivia and most service personnel expect to receive a small sum to keep for themselves. **Taxi drivers** are one of the few exceptions. They do not expect tips, although if you feel you would like to offer something then the best way is to round up the fare. If you hire a cab for several hours or a day then a tip would be appropriate – about 10% of the fare should do the trick. Locals tend to negotiate an all-in price for a day's taxi hire, in which case a tip on top wouldn't be appropriate. If you speak the language then this is something to consider. Bolivia's **hotels** and **restaurants** tend not to add a service charge. Instead, they expect diners to add a 10–15% gratuity to the cost of their meal if they have been happy with the experience. If there is a service charge then you are not expected to offer any further gratuity unless you wish to do so. You should also allow about 5–7Bs per bag for porters in hotels.

If you are invited to dine in a Bolivian home, take a small, good-quality gift for the hostess; beautifully wrapped chocolates or pastries are spot on. Punctuality isn't a prerequisite, although dressing quite smartly is. Bolivians do not take kindly to discussing business at social events, preferring to make separate appointments in their office or over lunch. Business gifts, such as items displaying a corporate logo, are given between colleagues. Anything more personal or expensive like whisky or electronic goods should be left until after a business agreement has been reached.

Brazil

🖃	**Currency**	Brazilian real (R$), BRL; R$1 = 100 centavos
🛏	**Hotels**	Porter R$2–3; Chambermaid R$2
🍴	**Restaurants**	10–15%
🚗	**Taxis**	No tip or 10%

Tipping is not usual, but always appreciated as wages for service personnel are often low. **Hotels** and **restaurants** usually include a service charge, called a *Taxa de serviço* or just *serviço*, but where this is not stipulated you can add a gratuity of around 15%. **Taxi drivers** don't tend to expect a tip, except in Rio, where drivers are worldly-wise and expect you to round up or add about 10%. Chambermaids and valets, to whom it is customary to give about R$2, cloakroom attendants (about the same), hairdressers and barbers (about 10%) and porters (about R$2–3 per bag, more in an upmarket hotel), are a few other service personnel you may wish to reward. Airport porters expect R$1–2 per bag. It is not customary to tip anyone who delivers something to you. If you are planning to take a guided trip during your time in Brazil, you'll probably find your **tour director** will be highly knowledgeable and bilingual. You'll need to give him or her about R$3–5 per day, and a little less for your driver.

In business, Brazilians like to take their time, enjoy lively conversation and really get to know you. While you may think that negotiations are getting nowhere you may be pleasantly surprised to find decisions have already been made – you'll just need to tie up any loose ends. Giving gifts in a business situation is not commonplace, but taking chocolate if visiting someone's home is always appreciated. Avoid wrapping presents in black or purple paper – these colours are reserved for mourning.

Chile

≋	**Currency**	Chilean peso ($), CLP; I peso = 100 centavos
⌑	**Hotels**	Porter 600 pesos; Chambermaid 500 pesos
⑪	**Restaurants**	10%
🚗	**Taxis**	Round up

Chile is a tad relaxed about tipping and who and what you tip is left very much to your discretion. The golden figure of 10% works well, and **restaurants** in particular would expect about this amount to be left if you were happy with the service. Some restaurants include a service charge so take a look at your bill before deciding how much to leave. In **hotels**, it's a good idea to have a few notes to hand to tip porters or doormen, typically around 600 pesos per bag. Doormen are usually given slightly more than porters.

If you are planning to take a **taxi** from the airport or for a tour of the city then you'll find your driver appreciates it if you round up the fare. If you feel the service has been especially good, for instance if your driver has shown you parts of the city and given you information, then you might like to leave as much as 20%. In cities, many of the cab drivers own their own vehicles and don't really expect a gratuity at all.

When giving gifts it is best to avoid dark colours; black and purple symbolise death. Ideal gifts for a hostess are brightly coloured flowers and baskets of fruit or sweets. In business, always wait until your relationship is on firm ground before offering a gift.

Colombia

✍ **Currency**	Colombian peso ($), COP; I peso = 100 centavos	
🏨 **Hotels**	Porter 500 pesos; Chambermaid 400 pesos	
🍴 **Restaurants**	10%	
🚗 **Taxis**	Round up	

Colombia is an exciting, multicultural country with dancing, music and fine cuisine all part of everyday life, and the number of visitors to the country's top tourist areas has increased significantly in recent years. There are **hotels** of all standards that cater for visitors, especially in the major cities of Bogotá, Cali and Medellín. In terms of service charges, most of the city establishments add about 15% to the bill, and although no further gratuity is expected it is unlikely to be refused if you wish to reward someone in particular for their attentive efforts. If you don't see that a service charge has been added leave about 10%, or 15% if in a high-end **restaurant**. You can also round up for convenience. In rural areas, service personnel do not expect a tip, even for exceptional service, but rounding up or adding about 5% is generally appreciated. Colombia's taxi drivers don't expect tips, although you may like to round up, and its hotel and airport porters tend to be looking to receive 500 pesos or so per item of luggage.

Business and dining out is all rather formal, and even dinner in someone's home with guests present is seldom casual. The giving of gifts is similar. Flowers are always appreciated, especially roses, and spirits from around the world make a good gift because they are so expensive in Colombia. Business gifts are given when the relationship is gaining in strength. All gifts are reciprocated and given the utmost respect.

Costa Rica

🐚	**Currency**	Costa Rican colón (₡), CRC; ₡1 = 100 céntimos
🛏	**Hotels**	Porter ₡500; Chambermaid ₡250–300
🍴	**Restaurants**	10%
🚕	**Taxis**	Round up

Not only will you enjoy some fine cuisine when dining out in a Costa Rican **restaurant**, but you'll also have a brief lesson in arithmetic. When you get your bill you'll find there's a 15% tax, plus a further 10% as a service charge. On top of this you are generally expected to tip by a further 10%. Although it is actually much cheaper than North America or Europe, Costa Rica can be a little on the expensive side for tourists depending on where you stay or eat, so don't forget to factor in the tips when you are working out your holiday budget.

Hotels add a similar amount for service, and you'll find that porters are always happy to assist with luggage for about ₡500 or so per bag, while chambermaids expect about ₡250–300 per day. **Taxi drivers**, on the whole, don't expect a tip, but rounding up the fare or simply adding about 10% will always be appreciated. The 10% unwritten rule applies equally well to **tour guides** and their **drivers**. The exception is if you've enjoyed a special interests trip, such as white-water rafting, when you might like to offer more than 10% to your guide in recognition of their expertise.

Business etiquette involves lengthy lunches and the giving of corporate logo-emblazoned gifts, while social entertaining, which is done with a flourish here, is almost always an evening affair. Gifts are appreciated – the best options are chocolates, whisky or a richly wrapped bouquet of flowers.

Ecuador

🛥	**Currency**	US dollar (US$), USD; US$1 = 100 cents
🛏	**Hotels**	Porter 50–75 cents; Chambermaid 50–75 cents
🍴	**Restaurants**	Service charge included, plus 5–10%
🚗	**Taxis**	Round up

Ecuador adopted the US dollar as its currency in March 2000, which makes it easy for visitors from the US, and even for travellers from other countries, as it makes deciding how much to tip a bit more straightforward. Ecuador is accustomed to tipping service personnel, and while there are no hard and fast rules there are a few basic standards. For instance, in **restaurants** you will almost always find there's a gratuity amount added to your bill, with a further 5–10% expected for good service. This additional tip is usually given directly to the waiter or waitress.

Hotel and **airport porters** should be tipped around 50–75 cents or so per bag, while your chambermaid ought to receive something in the region of US$1–2 per day of your stay.

As a rule, **taxi drivers** do not expect a tip at all, but will of course be appreciative if you choose to offer one – 10% works well, as does rounding up. The customary figure for **tour guides** hovers at around the US$5–6 per person per tour mark, but is always left to your discretion on how much you wish to offer.

You will find that Ecuadorians are a little formal in business, but hugely friendly and generous in a social environment. If dining with a local family, it is considered good form to take a small gift for the hostess. Choose wine or chocolates – nothing too outlandish or expensive, as otherwise your host or hostess may feel uncomfortable with your generosity.

Guyana

🪙	**Currency**	Guyana dollar (G$), GYD: G$1 = 100 cents
💵	**Hotels**	Porter G$100–200; Chambermaid no tip
🍴	**Restaurants**	10%
🚕	**Taxis**	No tip

In most cases tipping in Guyana has not become the standard and is not expected, but is appreciated if you're happy with the service. Georgetown's nicer **restaurants** – particularly those in the hotels favoured by international visitors – will add a service charge to the bill; if it is not, leave about a 10% tip. In smaller restaurants, **cafés** and bars tipping is not expected. In Georgetown **hotels**, tipping staff is discretionary. If a porter helps with your bags, something small is appreciated. If you're pleased with the chambermaid's service, leave a tip on the bed each day. In both cases, G$100–200 is plenty.

At interior lodges and resorts, where rates are typically inclusive of lodging, meals, and activities, it is customary to leave a tip with the manager or village captain for equal distribution amongst all staff involved. Depending on the overall service you receive, and bearing in mind that the tip will be for everybody both directly and indirectly involved in your visit, roughly 10% tip, or G$2,000–4,000 per day is adequate. For **guides** – either in the interior or in Georgetown – a 10% tip is sufficient. In the interior, tips are best in Guyanese dollars, as there are no facilities for exchanging money.

When visiting homes, tips or gifts are not expected. Guyanese hospitality is legendary, and people are more than happy to share it with visitors for nothing in return.

Panama

🖋 **Currency**		US dollar (US$), USD; US$1 = 100 cents. Also, the Panama balboa (B), PAB; B1 = 100 centésimos
🛏 **Hotels**		Porter no tip; Chambermaid no tip
🍴 **Restaurants**		10%
🚗 **Taxis**		Round up

Panama is one of the few countries that works on a double currency system. Technically, its currency is the balboa, but it adopted the US dollar many years ago and today runs the two simultaneously. Coinage tends to be the balboa, while notes are usually US dollars. Tipping is not traditional in Panama, but as the number of tourists increase year on year the practice has become more widespread. Some of the upmarket **restaurants** and **hotels** now expect diners to leave about 10%, although elsewhere it is left very much to the individual. Rounding up the bill by about 10% of the total is becoming the norm.

Some industry personnel still find the whole business of tipping a tad uncomfortable, and therefore don't expect you to pay any more than the agreed amount. **Taxi drivers** are a prime example. Of course, you might like to round up and it will always be appreciated if you do. It's a bit different with porters, who rely heavily on tips to bolster their often low incomes. Work on about US$2 per bag.

The giving of gifts is not commonplace, perhaps because Panamanians like nothing more than dining or just simply socialising in each other's homes most days. If a Panamanian befriends you and invites you to his or her home you won't be expected to bring a present. Nonetheless you should be polite and respectful, and of course engage in lively conversation.

Paraguay

🕮	**Currency**	Paraguayan guarani (Gs), PYG; Gs1
🛏	**Hotels**	Porter Gs5,000; Chambermaid Gs10,000
🍴	**Restaurants**	Service charge included, otherwise 10%
🚗	**Taxis**	Round up

Upmarket **hotels** and **restaurants** in Paraguay often add a service charge as standard, or at least make the recommendation that 10% be added. Not all do though, so check to gauge how much you wish to leave if you intend to tip. Hotel porters tend to expect about Gs5,000 per bag. Chambermaids are usually tipped by way of an add-on to the bill, although not every establishment does this. Around 10,000 guarani per day is an acceptable figure, especially if they have done a sterling job in keeping your room clean and tidy.

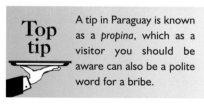

Top tip

A tip in Paraguay is known as a *propina*, which as a visitor you should be aware can also be a polite word for a bribe.

Taxi drivers, traditionally, have never expected a tip and it is usual to pay the exact fare displayed on the meter. Having said that, it is always appreciated if you decide to round up the fare as tips can help to boost an often low level of income. If your cab doesn't have a meter then you should agree a price before you travel. If you wish you can round up the agreed amount.

Paraguayans are friendly and accommodating hosts, so be sure to accept if you are invited to dine with a local family. You should dress reasonably smartly, but you will not be expected to arrive bang on time – the punctuality of *la hora paraguaya* is always in contrast to the prompt punctuality of *la hora inglesa* (English time). Take a bottle of wine as a gift. If, however, you are dining with a poor family, something edible would make a suitable gift. When you accept an invitation you could suggest bringing an *ensalada* (salad) or a *postre* (dessert), either of which would be ideal.

Peru

✎ **Currency**	Peruvian nuevo sol (S/.), PEN; S/.1 = 100 céntimos
🏨 **Hotels**	Porter S/.5; Chambermaid S/.5
🍽 **Restaurants**	Service charge 10%
🚗 **Taxis**	No tip

In most of the better **hotels** and **restaurants** in Peru, a 10% service charge is already included in the bill. Look for the words *propina* or *servicio*, which both indicate the addition of a gratuity. You could make it 5% or even 10% on top if the quality of service justifies it. Cheaper restaurants don't usually include a tip in the bill, leaving customers to give the waiters a going rate of 10%. For hotel porters, reckon on S/.15. Porters at airports or railway stations usually get around S/.20. A good hairdresser expects a 10–15% tip. It is customary to tip your **tour guide** and **bus driver** on a daily basis of S/.10 to S/.20 each per day, per person, depending on how you feel the service has been.

Taxis don't have meters in Peru so you should agree the fare before starting off. The cabbie will certainly have included a decent gratuity within the price. Nothing further is needed.

Many visitors head for Peru purely for the chance to walk along the Inca Trail. The **local guide**, **cook** and **porters** who will accompany you along the trail will need tipping. The porters especially carry incredible loads of luggage and equipment and have great knowledge of the mountains. They are an essential part of treks, but the reality of their working conditions comes as a shock. They often need the money to provide for their family, so you may feel it's good to be generous. According to Peruvian law, porters should receive a set minimum wage, but some do not. Pack animals

Top tip
If you are in Peru on business, it is worth remembering that punctuality is not a Peruvian trademark – your hosts may be anything up to an hour late for a scheduled appointment.

such as horses, mules and llamas are now banned from the trail so porters have to carry all the camping equipment – tents, dining tent, kitchen tent, tables, chairs, stove, gas bottle and food – maximum loads of 25kg, theoretically. A typical four-day group trek of 14 persons is conducted with 12 porters, the guide, his assistant and the cook. A general recommendation is that they should be tipped enough by the party to ensure that the guide takes home a collective tip of around S/.30 per person, cook S/.30 per person and each porter around S/.15 per person. If you have employed a personal porter then you'll pay his tip yourself.

Peruvians normally shake hands on meeting, and kiss acquaintances on the cheek. If visiting a Peruvian's home, it is customary to bring a small present for your host like a cake or a bottle of wine, or something from your home country. It is best to avoid bringing very lavish gifts, as this may make your host uncomfortable. Should you be invited to stay for a longer period of time, it is a good idea to try to repay your host in kind, for instance by helping out with grocery shopping.

Uruguay

🪙 **Currency**	Uruguayan peso ($), UYU; I peso = 100 centésimos	
🏨 **Hotels**	Porter 2 pesos; Chambermaid 2 pesos	
🍽 **Restaurants**	10%	
🚕 **Taxis**	Round up	

Tipping in hotels and restaurants, as well as to other service personnel, is not a major preoccupation in Uruguay, but is rather recognised as a discreet way of showing someone that you have appreciated their kindness and attentive service. As such, it is always best to round up a bill or give a tip directly to the person for whom you intended it as a thank you.

In **restaurants** and **hotels**, 10% is considered appropriate; any more and you are erring towards being impolite. **Taxi drivers** do not expect a tip as such, but it has become customary to round up the fare, while **tour guides** should receive around 5–10 pesos if they have been helpful to you. **Porters** are always happy to assist you with your luggage, and are almost always friendly, but of course they generally expect a small gratuity for their services; a couple of pesos per bag would be about right. US dollars are also accepted throughout Uruguay.

Uruguayans love to give each other gifts too, and if you, as a visitor, are invited to someone's home for dinner then take a small gift such as chocolates wrapped prettily in paper with bows. You may even like to send flowers, especially roses, in advance of the dinner date. Corporate gifts are exchanged between business colleagues, but anything more personal is really only given if a deal has been concluded.

Venezuela

💰 **Currency**	Venezuelan bolívar fuerte (Bs.F.), VEF;
	Bs.F.1 = 100 céntimos
🏨 **Hotels**	Porter Bs.F.2; Chambermaid Bs.F.2
🍴 **Restaurants**	10%
🚕 **Taxis**	10%

Most Venezuelans have hospitality down to a fine art, so you can usually be sure of many memorable times dining in the country's restaurants, with attentive and friendly waiting staff caring for your needs. In such situations you will probably wish to leave a gratuity, although do not feel obliged to do so if the service has not been friendly and efficient, which can still be the case. Some **restaurants** and **hotels** include a service charge in their pricing, while others prefer to leave tipping very much to the discretion of the customer. The norm is about 10%. You will find hotel porters look for about Bs.F.2 per bag, and if you indulge at a hairdresser's or barber's during your stay then expect to add about 10% to the bill. Similarly, **tour guides** tend to expect about 10% of the value you paid for your excursion. For **taxis**, agree the price with the driver before you leave, incorporating around 10% extra as the tip if you wish.

Venezuelans love to entertain friends. If you are invited to dinner consider it a huge honour. Always dress smartly, arrive on or after the appointed time, never before, and take a small gift of flowers, perhaps the national orchid, or confectionery. Coffee symbolises hospitality and is important in Venezuelan culture, so always accept a cup if it is offered to you. To decline may be seen as ungrateful.

North America and the Caribbean

It is common for many of the countries in North America and the Caribbean to add a service charge of between 10% and 15%. Canada is, perhaps, the exception, where levels are closer to those in the US, around 20%. Further gratuities are usually considered discretionary. The all-inclusive concept is especially popular in this region, where live entertainment and drinks are all part of the package, and no tipping is expected although always appreciated. Depending on the circumstances, tipping usually helps to smooth the way, but North Americans and Caribbean islanders are not avaricious.

Bahamas

🖉 **Currency**	Bahamian dollar (B$), BSD; B$1 = 100 cents	
🛏 **Hotels**	Porter B$1 per bag; Chambermaid B$2	
🍴 **Restaurants**	Service charge included	
🚗 **Taxis**	10–15%	

Knowing whether or not to tip is all rather straightforward in the Bahamas. **Taxis** operate to a fixed rate set by the government and if you let your driver know where you are going then you will be quoted for the journey. It may be just from the airport to your hotel, or you may fancy taking a taxi on a tour of the island. Either way, you'll know what the bill will be at the end. It's all very organised. You will then be expected to add about 10–15% on top as a gratuity for your driver, although of course only if he's done a grand job.

Hotels and **restaurants** are just as organised. Almost all will add 15% service charge on top of your bill, which is divided amongst staff. If you do find one that hasn't, and they are rare, just round up so it equates to about the same percentage. In some of the classiest hotels and restaurants you may even see a 20% service charge. Airport and hotel porters expect to receive B$1 or so per bag when they assist with your luggage, and chambermaids about B$2 per day.

Tipping in hard currency (usually US dollars, but British pounds sterling as well) is often more appreciated than local currency.

The Bahamas is fairly laidback when it comes to etiquette. Greet people with a handshake. If you are there on business, exchange business cards without any fuss. Don't move to a first-name basis unless prompted to do so by your host. If invited to dine with a family, arrive on time and well dressed, and bring a gift of fruits, flowers or wine.

Bermuda

🪙 **Currency**	Bermudan dollar (BD$), BMD; BD$1 = 100 cents	
🛎️ **Hotels**	Porter BD$1; Chambermaid BD$5–10	
🍴 **Restaurants**	Service charge included, otherwise 15%	
🚕 **Taxis**	10–15%	

A service charge is commonly added to **hotel** and **restaurant** bills, and thereby eliminating the need to tip waiting staff, porters, concierge personnel and chambermaids or valets individually. You will see an automatic charge of 10% to cover these services, and no further gratuity is considered necessary; however, if the chambermaid has kept your room well you might want to leave between BD$5–10. Similarly, if a staff member has gone out of their way for you then you may wish to offer a little something extra, for example if you have used the concierge often during your stay. Around BD$8–10 would be about right. Some restaurants may even go so far as adding 15% as a service charge, while others, curiously, prefer not to add anything and leave you to judge whether to tip. You may like to use the standard 15% as a guide in this situation. Other people you might want to tip are porters, to whom it is customary to give BD$1 a bag, and **taxi drivers**, who generally receive about 10–15% on top of the taxi fare to keep for themselves. The US dollar is also widely used.

Old-fashioned courtesy prevails; make the effort to greet people first before asking them questions of any sort. Business is fairly relaxed – many workplaces stipulate only 'business casual' rather than suits. Strive to be on time for meetings. If you are invited to a Bermudan family's house for dinner, flowers and a bottle of wine make an ideal gift.

Canada

&#x2040;	**Currency**	Canadian dollar (C$), CAD; C$1 = 100 cents
&#x1F3E8;	**Hotels**	Porter C$1–2; Chambermaid C$2
&#x1F37D;	**Restaurants**	15–20%
&#x1F695;	**Taxis**	15–20%

Like the US, Canada became immersed in the culture of tipping many years ago and providing that Canadians receive an excellent service they are happy to tip as much as 20% of the total value paid for most services. In a **restaurant**, for instance, a 20% tip is the norm for waiters and waitresses, and even the bartender, which is given directly in cash. However, you aren't expected to tip if eating at the counter (not that such a tip would be turned down!). If checking in your coat then a dollar is offered to the cloakroom attendant. Some **hotels** include a service charge in their quoted price, in which case it is unnecessary to tip anything further to room staff. If not, reckon on around C$2 a day for your chambermaid. It is customary to tip your porter too; allow C$1–2 per bag.

When out and about, expect to add about 20% to the cost of your taxi fare, and a similar amount divided between your **tour guide and driver** if taking a coach excursion.

Gifts tend not to be given in business situations until a relationship is firmly established and successful negotiations have taken place. Shake hands and give your business card at the start of a meeting. If invited to someone's home to dine take a good bottle of wine, accompanied by a box of beautifully decorated handmade chocolates if you are feeling generous.

Cayman Islands

🐚 **Currency**	Cayman Islands dollar (CI$), KYD; CI$1 = 100 cents	
🛏 **Hotels**	Porter CI$2; Chambermaid CI$1–2	
🍴 **Restaurants**	Service charge usually included	
🚕 **Taxis**	15%	

Tipping in the Cayman Islands is all part of the experience and everyone, from serving staff to drivers, expects a show of appreciation. The norm is between 10% and 15%, and sometimes as high as 20%, because of the strong American influence. Some **hotels** and **restaurants** add a service charge to their bills, but it is worth checking to gauge if and how much to leave. Some of the smaller hotels and condo-style establishments prefer to let the guest choose, and do not add a charge to the bill. Do not confuse a service charge with the 10% tax imposed on all hotel rooms.

Other service personnel you might come into contact with are **taxi drivers** who will charge you a fixed government-controlled fare that does not include a gratuity. The standard is 15% to the driver if you have been pleased with the journey, and whether he or she has been helpful and friendly. You may go on excursions during your time on the islands, or go out on one of the many dive boats, in which case a 10% or so tip should do the trick.

The traditional pace of life in the Cayman Islands is slow and relaxed, but manners are of a high standard; older women are generally addressed as 'ma'am' or 'Miss' (plus their first name), and older men as 'sir'. On the business front, the norm is to wear suits for meetings and formal occasions, with a handshake the usual greeting. If visiting someone's house for dinner, simply do as you do at home – flowers and a bottle of wine are ideal.

Cuba

🪙 **Currency**	Cuban peso ($ or $MN), CUP; 1P = 100 centavos. Also Cuban convertible peso (CUC$), CUC; CUC$1 = 100 centavos	
🛏 **Hotels**	Porter CUC$1; Chambermaid CUC$1	
🍴 **Restaurants**	10–20%	
🚕 **Taxis**	Round up	

Cuba's spirited people are always ready to help you, although wages are very low and those who work in the service industry rely heavily on tips left by satisfied customers. It's a balancing act as to whether you tip the going rate and avoid any possibility of causing offence or whether you add a bit extra if it will ultimately help someone have a better day. Generally speaking, **hotels** and **restaurants**, most of which are government-run, should not add a service charge because it is not the done thing, but in reality many do. It is easiest just to pay as part of the bill any 'service charge' and to tip the actual waitress or waiter directly – 10% or more for exceptional service. As a guide, the convertible peso, CUC, is worth between a US dollar and a euro. There are no actual US dollars traded in Cuba, and a common

Cuba's has two official currencies: the Cuban peso (CUP) and the Cuban convertible peso (CUC). Cubans are paid in CUP and use it to buy staple goods. The CUC, on the other hand, is used for tourism and more expensive items. Both are closed currencies; you will have to exchange your money when you arrive in Cuba. Tips should be made in Cuban convertible pesos.

Top tip

mistake is to see the '$' sign on price tags and imagine that a purchase can be made in this currency. For hotel chambermaids consider giving a few convertible pesos per day, or a present, and the same for porters per bag. You may also like to consider the same for other people who assist you, or quite a bit more, for example CUC$10–20 per day, for **drivers** or **guides**.

The giving of gifts is prevalent in Cuba, as many basic to luxury items are hard to find. Take a selection of goodies, such as chocolate or toiletries, from home to give as gifts. If invited to dine with a Cuban family, you may like to take toys if your host or hostess has children, as these can be in short supply, as are paper items like exercise books, sketch books, writing paper and cards.

Dominica

Tipping in Dominica is considered normal service practice and you will almost always see around 10% already added to your **restaurant** or **hotel** bill. Leaving extra tips for good service, although discretionary, is encouraged by proprietors. Reckon on an additional 5% if the service charge is included, and 15% if it is not.

It is also customary to tip hotel room service personnel the equivalent US$4–5, which equates to around EC$12, and bellboys and **porters** about the same per item of luggage. It is not necessary to tip **taxi drivers** as fares in Dominica are set by the government; however, if your driver has been especially helpful with information or has carried your bags for you it is acceptable to offer a little something for his trouble. Keep it in line with what you would tip hotel staff and you will be about right. If your taxi driver acts as a guide by showing you the island then consider about 10% of the cost of the trip for a gratuity. Ditto for a boat charter.

Business processes can sometimes seem a little awkward and old-fashioned, and in the heat and humidity it is easy to get a little hot under the collar. If invited to dinner by a Dominican it's nice to bring a gift, although by no means expected. Locals often take produce from their garden when visiting friends or relatives. As visitors cannot really do that, something nice from home that is hard to get hold of on the islands, such as a good bottle of wine or single malt whisky, or some expensive chocolates, will always be very welcome.

Dominican Republic

🪙 **Currency**	Dominican peso (RD$), DOP; RD$1 = 100 centavos	
🛎 **Hotels**	Porter RD$10; Chambermaid RD$30	
🍴 **Restaurants**	Service charge included	
🚕 **Taxis**	10%	

Most of Spanish-speaking Dominican Republic's resorts are built for an international clientele with the all-inclusive 'club' concept being especially popular. In such hotels and resorts, staff members are paid a normal local wage and no tipping is expected. In practice, most visitors are happy to express thanks with gratuities here and there. Leave a US dollar bill or RD$30 each day for the chambermaid, same to the barman, and RD$100 to the waiter and you'll get prime service, but there's no obligation. On paid-for excursions, **guides** and **drivers** appreciate the equivalent of a US$1 each. For hotel-based **taxi drivers**, no extra tipping is necessary.

In city **hotels** used by businessmen and independent tourists, an automatic 10% service charge is levied, although it doesn't necessarily reach the staff. **Restaurants** add an obligatory 10% service charge, plus 16% sales tax to bills. The waiter service (which is normally good) is rewarded with a tip of 5–10%. Porters hope to receive RD$10 per bag. Maids are usually tipped around RD$30 each day.

Regular licensed **taxis** do not have meters. Airports and some hotels display agreed rates to standard destinations and your journey will be charged according to the number of kilometres you travel, otherwise you need to agree a fare with the driver, who then expects 10% on top. For relaxed sightseeing or business calls with

Top tip It is worth noting that tipping in hard currency (usually US dollars, but British pounds sterling as well) is often appreciated more than local currency.

stops here and there it's worth negotiating an hourly or all-day rate. You'll probably be quite happy to add a bit extra at the end.

The giving of gifts is widely practised in the Dominican Republic and always appreciated, whether it be in the home or a business environment. Pastries, chocolates or a craft item from your country is always welcomed. Always dress smartly if invited for dinner.

Always arrive on time to meetings if you are in the Dominican Republic on business. You should present your business card, and show respect when receiving your associates' cards. Business cards are considered an important aspect of a business relationship.

Grenada, Carriacou & Petite Martinique

&#x26C4;	**Currency**	East Caribbean dollar (EC$), XCD; EC$1 = 100 cents
&#x1F6CF;	**Hotels**	Porter EC$10–20; Chambermaid EC$10–20
&#x1F37D;	**Restaurants**	10–15%
&#x1F697;	**Taxis**	Round up

Grenada, Petite Martinique and Carriacou rely heavily on tourism, and what service personnel earn during the high season months may have to last them once the visitors have gone. With that in mind, adding around US$10, equal to about EC$28, to a **restaurant** bill might, to a local person, mount up and make relatively low wages go much further. The islands in this part of the Caribbean Sea are popular stop off points for cruiseships, and as the onboard guests come ashore, so tips become more plentiful. With that in mind, you may find that waiters expect a tip as a matter of course, although most will provide you with a good service regardless. It is good to show appreciation, however. As a guide, add 10–15% to **hotel** and **room** bills, and round up a taxi driver's fare to a similar percentage.

Greet people you meet on the islands with a smile and a handshake, just as you would do back home. Bringing gifts to dinner isn't really expected, but will be appreciated nonetheless. Your hosts will appreciate something from your home country which is difficult to obtain on the islands.

Jamaica

&#x1F6C9;	**Currency**	Jamaican dollars (J$), JMD; J$1 = 100 cents
&#x1F3E8;	**Hotels**	Porter J$50; Chambermaid J$35 (check the hotel doesn't ban tipping)
&#x1F37D;	**Restaurants**	Service charge included, otherwise 10–15%
&#x1F695;	**Taxis**	10%

Visiting this beautiful Caribbean island with its supremely friendly people, cuisine enriched with spices and juices and a lifestyle that revolves around music and having fun, will be a memory that will last a lifetime and the efficiency of Jamaican waiting staff adds to the experience. You will find that **hotel** and **restaurant** bills usually include a 10–15% service charge, and while there is no need to tip further you might like to round up or add J$100 or so for exceptional service, especially at the more upmarket locations. Tipping when a service charge is included is always considered to be at your discretion: likewise, if no service charge is included, which is a little rarer. In this case you may wish to leave a bit extra.

Porters generally expect a small tip. Around J$50 per bag is about right, perhaps bordering on the generous. **Taxi** drivers expect about 10% on top of the fare; if taking a taxi late at night or on a bank holiday, you may want to tip a little more, perhaps even double. Chambermaids tend to be tipped according to the service they provide. If it is good and they have kept your room in tip-top condition during your stay you might like to tip about J$75 per day. Leave it to the end of your stay and tip them personally. While tipping almost always helps to smooth the way, you will find many **hotels** and resorts in Jamaica operate on an all-inclusive basis and have a strict no-tipping policy – it's actually banned. If you are in any doubt about policy, ask at the hotel/resort reception, or your holiday rep. It

For a great holiday souvenir, look out for the colourfully dressed Jamaican women with fruit baskets full to the brim on their heads. They can often be seen in tourist areas. While you may think they are on their way to market or are trying to sell the fruit, they are in fact hoping for a few dollars from tourists keen to take a souvenir photograph.

Top tip

The result is usually well worth a tip. Remember these women may have several young mouths to feed at home, which may be a consideration for you when deciding how much to offer.

is also worth knowing that tips can be made in US dollars as well as the local currency – both are appreciated. During your stay you may take a **tour**. These are generally offered by your holiday company, in which case no tipping is necessary for your guide or driver, but if you negotiate with a tour company directly then offer about 10% on top of the price of the tour as a gratuity.

Jamaicans like to invite visitors to share a meal with them, which will usually be informal, friendly and relaxed. There is no real protocol for giving gifts, but something from your own country, such as a craft item or cosmetics, is always welcomed. In business, it is important to offer your card and talk in a straightforward manner to gain trust.

Mexico

🖉 **Currency**	Mexican peso (Mex$), MXN; Mex$1 = 100 centavo. US dollars (US$) also widely accepted; US$1 = 100 cents	
🏨 **Hotels**	Porter Mex$10; Chambermaid Mex$10	
🍴 **Restaurants**	10–15%	
🚕 **Taxis**	No tip	

If you're on a package tour, ignore freelance porters at the arrival airport who pretend to be the company's employees and will expect a hefty tip for taking your bags to your transport bus. Similarly, if you are an independent traveller it's a good idea to use an official **airport porter** and give him a Mex$10 tip per bag. The porter will escort you to the shared limousine service which will deliver you to your hotel at a low-cost set tariff with no haggling or tipping involved.

In Mexico, tipping is a national sport. Workers in the service industries depend on tips to boost their nominal basic wage. At **hotels** and **restaurants**, the percentage system is normal for drinks and meals. The standard is 10–15%, although visitors from the US where tipping is more generous have caused the Mexican locals to expect higher amounts. A key phrase on restaurant menus and bills is 'Propina no incluida' – 'Tip not included'. If in doubt, ask. However, some resort high-grade hotels and restaurants have switched to a 10–15% service charge, while waiters still hope for an additional 5% or at least a rounding up of the bill. Many catering staff think in US dollars. For instance, porters know that their counterparts in America average around US$2 per bag so they expect the peso equivalent from foreigners. Half that figure – Mex$10 – is OK, however. Many 'all-inclusive' resort hotels follow a no-tipping policy; everything's covered in the holiday cost so the porters don't hover

Top tip

One of the greatest compliments anyone can give you in Mexico is to invite you to their home for dinner. Remember, though, that the main meal of the day is served between 13.00 and 16.00. It is a good idea to take a gift for your host, such as chocolates, but if bringing flowers be sure to avoid the colour purple as it is commonly seen at funerals.

for a tip. If, however, your favourite waiter or chambermaid has been really friendly and helpful then a tip is not out of line. Chambermaids would expect a tipping basis of Mex$10 per day.

On sightseeing trips, the **driver** and **guide** appreciate a Mex$10–20 banknote for a half-day circuit, with this amount scaled up for a whole day tour or one lasting several days. It's not the custom to tip **taxi drivers**, but if a cabbie helps with your luggage then you might like to offer Mex$5–10. Among the other incidentals, petrol station attendants expect Mex$3–5, or more if they check oil and tyres. Parking attendants should be tipped Mex$5–10. For valet-parking service, reckon on Mex$10.

Mexico is well versed in business etiquette. In cementing a business relationship, the exchange of gifts is an established custom, especially at holiday times and in the period between 12 December (Virgin of Guadalupe Day) and Christmas Day. Ideal gifts are liqueurs or whisky, wines, fine food hampers or electronic equipment.

Puerto Rico

🖎	**Currency**	US dollar (US$), USD; US$1 = 100 cents
🛏	**Hotels**	Porter US$1–2; Chambermaid US$1–2
🍴	**Restaurants**	Service charge included, otherwise 15–20%
🚗	**Taxis**	15–20%

Puerto Ricans often refer to their currency as a *peso*, made up of 100 *chavitos*, but if you hear this in a restaurant, for instance, don't be confused as they're still referring to the US dollar and its 100 cents. **Restaurants** usually, but not always, add a service charge to their pricing, and no further tip is expected. If it's not, then a tip of 15–20% is the norm. **Hotels**, similarly, add 10–15% automatically. You will find that it is customary to tip porters. A dollar or so per bag is about right. Chambermaids usually receive about US$1 per day of your stay, or perhaps US$2 if they have made just that little bit more effort and are helpful.

When out and about you'll find **taxi drivers** are keen to help with your bags and make your journey that extra bit special by giving you lots of information on their country. It may be genuinely free, of course, but they are probably hoping for a tip at the end of the journey too. It is customary to tip about 15–20% of the taxi fare.

If you choose to give a gift to someone who has helped you or to the hostess if you are invited to dine in the home of a Puerto Rican family, then take flowers, or better still something edible like chocolate, sweets or pastries. Wrap them beautifully but don't be surprised if they are not unwrapped until after you have left – unwrapping a gift in public is considered extremely impolite.

Turks & Caicos Islands

🪙	**Currency**	US dollar (US$), USD; US$1 = 100 cents
🏨	**Hotels**	Porter US$1; Chambermaid US$1
🍴	**Restaurants**	Service charge included or 10–15%
🚕	**Taxis**	10–15%

Tipping is considered normal practice in the Turks and Caicos Islands. In **restaurants** around 15% is frequently added to the bill, so even if you have had a great meal you might just like to check and if a gratuity is noted then you can decide how much more, if any, you wish to leave. It is best to give any extra tip directly to the person who has given you good service, and in cash. The same can be said for **hotel** staff, as a tip left at the end of your stay may be distributed amongst all the staff and not necessarily be given to the one person who has made your stay that little bit more pleasurable.

Other personnel you might like to tip are porters at the rate of around US$1 per bag, chambermaids about the same per day and **guides** that you may encounter on leisure activities, such as on a diving or horse-riding excursion. Allow around 10% of the price you paid for the activity.

Taxi drivers generally do a great job in showing you the sights and giving you lots of local information, but are not always doing so for a gratuity, although it should be noted that this isn't the case for

Top tip

It is not necessary to tip the drivers of communal people-carrier taxis picking up from the airport and dropping off at various hotels, or those taking passengers from the ferry port in Grand Turk into town.

Provo, where 90% of tourists go. Until recently it was quite rare to tip a taxi driver at all. A good guide is to round up the fare by 10% to 15% of the bill.

Etiquette when invited to someone's home for dinner or in a business environment is quite formal until a relationship has formed. Take pastries or a good bottle of wine for your dinner host, but it is not necessary to take a gift to a business meeting.

USA

◈	**Currency**	US dollar (US$), USD; US$1 = 100 cents
▥	**Hotels**	Porter US$1–2; Chambermaid US$1–2
¶¶	**Restaurants**	15–20%
🚗	**Taxis**	15–20%

The US embraced the tipping culture many years ago, and Americans expect to tip anyone who provides a good service. If the service is poor then they will not. Waiters and waitresses, bartenders, taxi or hotel courtesy car drivers, barbers and hairdressers, and tour guides all tend to be tipped around 15% of the total bill. Expectations are rising though, and often you can look at a 20% tip, especially if you are feeling generous. **Hotels** do not usually include a service charge, although many operate plans whereby guests can pay upfront to eat in a variety of restaurants. Sometimes these plans include tax and gratuities, although most do not, so it is left to the individual to pay any extra. Similarly, **restaurants** tend not to include a service charge, but if they do it should always be clearly marked. If in doubt, the best thing is to ask and be sure of exactly what it is you are paying for.

Other people you may wish to tip include **porters** in hotels and at airports, who expect around US$1 per item of luggage, more if

Top tip

In restaurants, Americans often work on the basis that if you over-tip you will be remembered next time you are in. It's not a bad policy, but for a visitor it may be a waste of money unless you are 'in town' for many days and plan to use the same restaurant several times.

you have large or heavy bags. It is worth knowing that the help from Amtrak's 'Red Cap' porters at train stations is officially free, but most people still tip US$1–2 per item. On board a train, tips are generally given to waiters and bar staff as you would in conventional restaurants and bars. Chambermaids look to receive US$1–2 per night if your stay is for several days' duration, while cloakroom attendants generally receive US$2–5 when you collect your coat. People who open doors for you in hotels or restaurants may expect US$1–2 gratuity, as do people who park your car, those who wash or valet it, fill your car with fuel, shine your shoes, deliver your pizza, treat you at a spa or care for you at a casino or sports club. The maître d' in your upmarket restaurant is also likely to be tipped. If you are on business, tipping the maître d' may ensure a good table and attentive service, which you may think is worth it to impress your guests. Do not, however, try to tip government officials or public service personnel as this may be construed as a bribe.

Americans love to give gifts, especially when dining or partying in friends' homes. Flowers are always acceptable as a gift for the hostess, but do avoid white lilies or chrysanthemums as these are considered funeral flowers. Promotional gifts, such as stationery or gadgets with companies' logos and contact details clearly marked, tend to be given in business situations, with more personal items reserved for Christmas. Gifts are generally opened immediately.

Top tip

It's a good idea to keep a few notes, known as 'bills', ready for tipping, not only in hotels and restaurants, but for when you are out and about too. Tips should always be given discreetly.

Cruising

A regular topic of discussion among cruise passengers is tips: who should get them, how much should be offered and how should they be disbursed? Although virtually all ships give onboard advice via the front office or the cruise director, it's often difficult to track down guidance before booking a cruise.

The tipping recommendations of the world's leading cruise lines are summarised in this chapter. For ease of comparison, all guidance is expressed in US dollars, which is the most popular currency used on board for worldwide cruising. The aim is to give prospective passengers a better idea of the real overall cost.

How to tip on a cruise

Cruise lines' tipping systems are apt to confuse first-time cruisers and seasoned seafarers alike. There are still grey areas where tips are optional and made at guests' discretion. The task is made tougher because of a growing trend away from handing out direct cash tips to staff who have given you personal service. Many ships now offer 'freestyle cruising' or 'personal choice dining', which means guests can float between several restaurants, and therefore no longer have a regular waiter, waiter's assistant or wine waiter to reward.

One answer is to add an overall fixed sum to the shipboard account to cover tips for distribution among the personnel involved, which will mainly be the cabin and waiting staff. Other instances where you might find yourself considering a gratuity is if you use the casino and feel the croupier has served you well, you allow porters to assist you with luggage on and off the boat, and if you take sightseeing tours when in port and tip the guide and driver. In the cause of flexibility, travellers can ask the front desk to raise or lower the overall amount charged and can indicate the amount each staff sector should get from the total. Alternative ways of dealing with tips is to pay your booking agent in advance or to place cash in envelopes and give them to the staff member of your choice.

Some cruise lines include all gratuities in the package price, although for competitive reasons most are reluctant to follow that path as it would make their brochure prices appear higher. If tips are not included in the overall price, the average recommendation for onboard gratuities is US$10–15 per person per day. In addition to this, you will find there is usually a 15% gratuity added on to bar or spa bills.

Top tip

American Safari Cruises

🖱 www.americansafaricruises.com

The policy for gratuities on board the company's fleet of small cruiseships that sail the waters around Alaska, Hawaii, the Pacific Northwest and Mexico is that it is entirely discretionary. The company prides itself on a high level of customer care and, as such, it regards tipping as unnecessary as all staff are expected to take care of guests' every need efficiently and with a smile. However, the company acknowledges that guests who receive over and above an excellent experience may wish to offer a gratuity to individual staff members, and welcomes this initiative. Like most cruise companies, American Safari Cruises operates a shipboard account for making purchases.

Azamara Cruises

🖱 www.azamaracruises.com

This company has created a policy for gratuities which it feels offers the most convenience to passengers. It operates a multiple open-seating dining arrangement and, as such, passengers are likely to be served by many different members of staff. It includes gratuities for stateroom attendants, restaurant waiting staff and bar staff. The company automatically adds 18% gratuities for spa services. It recommends further gratuities to tour directors at the rate of US$5 per guest per day. The policy applies to all ships sailing the waters of the Caribbean, Europe, Asia, South America, Mexico, along the Panama Canal and transatlantic routes.

Cruising

Carnival Cruise Lines

🖱 www.carnival.com

All passengers automatically have US$10 per day added to their 'Sail and Sign' charge account. The amount is split between the cabin stateroom steward and staff, who get US$3.50, the dining room teams, who receive a total of US$5.50, and the remainder distributed between the kitchen and hotel services staff. The amounts can be adjusted at the purser's office dependent on the individual traveller's feelings about the quality of service. Bar tabs automatically include a 15% service charge. You are free to tip room-service staff, the maître d' and any other members of staff based upon the level of service you receive.

Celebrity Cruises

🖱 www.celebritycruises.com

The company automatically adds US$11.50 per person per day to the Seapass account of stateroom guests, US$12 for Concierge Class guests and US$15 for guests staying in suites. This covers gratuities for restaurant and stateroom staff who serve you during the cruise. These tips are split between the waiters at US$3.50 each, US$2.10 for the assistant waiter, US$1 for the dining room management team, US$3.50 for the butler in suites and stateroom personnel (US$4 in Concierge class and Aqua Class) and US$1.25 for all other staff. A standard 15% service charge is added to bar drinks. It's then up to you should you wish to offer gratuities for spa services, in the casino and to any other members of staff, such as bellboys.

Cruising

Costa Cruises

🖱 **www.costacruises.co.uk**

Gratuities for all hotel services are automatically charged to guests' Costa Card accounts on board the company's fleet of ships. The fees vary according to the ship, its destination and the itinerary, but typically will be US$10 per guest per day on Caribbean cruises and US$8 per guest per day on South American cruises and transoceanic cruises. Payment is required at the end of the cruise, as is customary. If you are planning to pay by credit card then advance notice must be given; if by cash then you will be required to leave a deposit. According to the company, the service charge is regarded as an integral part of the total price of the cruise. It cannot be altered, but you are not expected to offer any other tips on board unless you choose to do so for exceptional service.

Crystal Cruises

🖱 **www.crystalcruises.com**

Crystal Cruises regards tipping as a personal matter, and although it does not include gratuities in its cruise fares, does expect tips to be paid to staff. These can be prepaid or added to the guest's shipboard account. Suggested amounts per guest per day are US$5 for the cabin steward or stewardess (US$6 for single occupancy), along with US$5 for the senior waiter and US$3 for his or her assistant. Clients staying in Penthouse Suites should, it is suggested, tip US$5 per guest per day to the butler. Gratuities to the maître d', assistant steward or stewardess and night room-service personnel is left to guests'

Cruising

discretion. For guests dining in the onboard speciality restaurants, the waiting staff expect to receive around a US$7 tip paid directly, per person per dinner. All bar beverages are charged a gratuity of 15% automatically, while for spa services the company suggests a gratuity of 15% be added to the tab, although this is entirely discretionary.

Cunard Line

🖱 **www.cunard.com**

Gratuities are automatically added to guests' shipboard accounts for dining room waiters, cabin steward and other staff. The 'Hotel and Dining charge' is applied daily. Rates per person, including children, are US$14 for accommodation with grill dining and US$12 for passengers who dine in all other restaurants. You will need to discuss any adjustments with the front desk. Bar or salon tabs have the standard 15% charge added to your bill. If you feel specific members of staff have shown you an especially high level of service then you are free to tip in cash directly when you feel it's appropriate.

Disney Cruise Line

🖱 **www.disneycruiseline.com**

It is customary to give gratuities to members of the staff on the themed Disney Cruise Line cruises, especially if they have shown you a high level of service. The company prefers not to automatically add charges, except in the case of 15% to bar, wine, beverage and deck service accounts, but offers the following suggestions for amounts to tip staff. Gratuities can be added to your onboard account if you wish for convenience. Typically on a three-night cruise you would be expected to tip a total of US$36 per person per cruise, split four ways, with US$12 going to the dining room server, US$9 to the dining room assistant server and US$3 for the dining room head server. The remaining US$12 is for the stateroom host or hostess. For four-night cruises the total suggested sum is US$48 and for a seven-night cruise US$84, both of which are divided for key staff in similar proportions. You are free to tip other staff such as the dining room manager, room-service personnel and for services in the spa or salon at your discretion, although a gratuity is not generally expected for babysitting services. Before the end of the cruise guests will receive a gratuity form and envelopes in which to place the individual amounts of cash. Passengers who prefer these tips to be charged to their shipboard account can complete the form and hand it into the guest services office. Receipts are usually given to place in the gratuity envelopes.

easyCruise

⌁ www.easycruise.com

The price you pay with easyCruise is for the cruise itself, and not things like food and beverages, spa treatments and additional housekeeping services over and above those specified prior to booking. The same goes for tips. The giving of gratuities and their amount is left entirely to the discretion of guests, so if you have received exceptional service from any members of staff then you are free to reward them in cash accordingly.

Cruising

Fred Olsen Cruises

🖱 www.fredolsencruises.com

Cruise prices do not include gratuities for cabin or restaurant staff on board, or for drivers and guides on any trips while ashore. The company says it is confident every guest will enjoy their onboard cruise experience and will wish to make a gratuity to staff members who have shown them a particularly high level of service. Tips are therefore entirely at the discretion of individual passengers, but as a guide you should look at giving around US$3 per guest per day to key personnel such as the cabin stewardess and restaurant waiter.

Hapag-Lloyd Cruises

🖱 www.hl-cruises.com

Hapag-Lloyd Cruises is confident guests will enjoy their experience on board its fleet of cruiseships and feels suggestions for what gratuities to offer staff members is unnecessary. Tipping is not expected, but if guests wish to reward exceptional service they can. Offering a gratuity and its amount is entirely at the guests' discretion.

Hebridean Island Cruises

🖱 www.hebridean.co.uk

This small ship cruise specialist prides itself on its all-inclusive policy. Everything from dining and drinks to the use of sports equipment and tour guides is included. Gratuities to staff are also included; in fact, the company says it actively discourages any form of tipping to ensure guests have the most pleasurable experience possible.

Holland America Line

www.hollandamerica.com

An automatic hotel service charge of US$11 per guest per day is added to onboard accounts for key cabin and restaurant staff, such as the stateroom steward or stewardess and waiters. A percentage of this charge to 'behind the scenes' staff who guests may never see, such as to those who work tirelessly in the kitchen or in the laundry. The figure can be adjusted at the end of the cruise. The normal 15% service charge is added to beverage bills in the bar or restaurant.

Hurtigruten ASA

www.hurtigruten.com

Hurtigruten operates a Cruisecard system on board. Although not compulsory, the company does recommend that its passengers take advantage of the system. A cash or credit-card deposit secures its use, and all payments, including gratuities, can be made on board using the card. Gratuities can also, of course, be made in cash. The company does not offer guidance on gratuity amounts, preferring to leave the decision to individuals on who they tip and by how much, depending on the service they have received.

Mediterranean Shipping Cruises

www.msccruises.com

It is customary to tip staff on board who have given a good personal service, although this shipping line advises different amounts for its

Cruising

European, Caribbean and other cruise destinations. On European cruises the company adds around US$12 per guest to passengers' accounts per day, although it emphasises that the gratuity is discretionary and should individuals wish to make adjustments then this is possible at the reception desk during the cruise. The guidelines suggested for Caribbean and some Mediterranean sailings are US$12 and US$6 for South American cruises, both per guest per day. A gratuity for bar staff is included in the drink prices, and cash tips for spa and casino personnel or anyone who has shown exceptional service can be made at the passenger's sole discretion.

Noble Caledonia

🖱 **www.noble-caledonia.co.uk**

Specialising in cruises that are educational and adventurous, Noble Caledonia has a fleet of sea and river vessels that sail to such places as Antarctica, Madagascar and the Galápagos Islands. Its gratuity policy varies according to the tour or vessel chosen, but passengers will be advised of what is included prior to departure. Where gratuities are not included in the price the company stresses tipping is discretionary, but suggests around £1–£2 (US$1.60–3.20) per bag for porters, £5–£10 (US$8–16) per passenger per day for onboard crew, and if taking an excursion about £2 (US$3.20) per day for your local guide and £1 (US$1.60) per day for the driver. On occasion the tour manager may organise a collective pool of tips from passengers for onboard staff. It also advises that in some instances a vessel's policy is to add a service charge to your onboard account automatically, but you can opt not to pay this.

Norwegian Cruise Line

🖰 www.ncl.com

The company operates a scheme whereby a US$12 per guest per day service charge is automatically added to onboard accounts, which is distributed amongst staff who work behind the scenes as well as restaurant waiting staff and stateroom stewards. It can be prepaid when making a booking. The charge is applicable to all guests aged three years and over. If you wish to tip more or less than the suggested guideline, you can contact the front desk to make adjustments. In addition, the company states that should guests wish to offer individual staff members a gratuity then it is happy for them to do so. For bar staff a tip of 15% is recommended and for spa staff 18%. The company says it encourages staff to 'go the extra mile' and, in turn, permits its team to accept cash tips.

Ocean Village Cruises

🖰 www.oceanvillageholidays.co.uk

Basic tips are included in the price, but the company recognises that passengers may wish to offer further gratuities to staff members and says it is an acceptable practice on its ships. Such tips are discretionary and tend to be presented in cash on the last night of the cruise.

Oceania Cruises

🖰 www.oceaniacruiseline.com

Owing to the open-dining nature of Oceania, gratuities are added to clients' onboard accounts at US$13 per person per day. For clients

Cruising

booked into a suite, an additional daily US$6 per person covers tips for the butler service. These suggestions, says Oceania Cruises, apply to its *Insignia*, *Nautica*, *Marina* and *Regatta* ships and can be raised or lowered at the front desk at passengers' discretion. Gratuities of 18% are automatically added to bar charges and spa services.

Oceanwide Expeditions

🖱 **www.oceanwide-expeditions.com**

Specialising in expedition-style cruises to places like Antarctica, Oceanwide Expeditions provides a whole host of support services. These are tailored so guests may enjoy activities such as glacier walking or kayaking. The company recognises that passengers may like to reward staff members, but prefers that gratuities and their amounts be entirely discretionary.

Orient Lines

🖱 **www.orientlines.com**

Orient Lines prides itself on having a dedicated Filipino staff which regards providing an attentive service as nothing less than a privilege. However, the company is happy for its staff to receive gratuities. The amount is entirely discretionary, but Orient Lines suggests around US$9 per person per day, split so as to reward your cabin steward, your waiter and bus boy. Tips should be distributed in cash or travellers' cheques at the end of the cruise. Additional gratuities may be given if the service has been exceptional, and is of course at each passenger's sole discretion. A 15% service charge is added to tabs for drinks, beauty and spa treatments.

P&O Cruises

🖱 www.pocruises.com

This company, which offers cruises around the world, has two styles of tipping. For guests on its Freedom Dining option the company advises that £1.60 (around US$2.50) is added per person per day to guests' shipboard accounts, which will be divided amongst restaurant staff. The sum can be increased or decreased at reception during the cruise. Further gratuities to, for example, stateroom stewards, may be given in cash. Guests not on the Freedom Dining option are advised to offer gratuities in cash. Recommended amounts are £3.10 (approximately US$5) per person over 12 years of age per day for restaurant and stateroom stewards. Sums given over this are entirely at the guests' discretion.

Princess Cruises

🖱 www.princess.com

An automatic US$11 for suites and mini-suites, and US$10.50 for all other staterooms per person per day (including children) is added to passengers' onboard accounts on all Princess cruises. The amount may be raised or lowered at the front desk during the cruise, and is shared fairly amongst restaurant stewards, stateroom stewards, kitchen staff and the laundry team. This is aimed at saving passengers the worry of having to decide who to tip and by how much. The spa and casino teams do not benefit from the gratuities policy and the company suggests passengers may like to reward key members of the teams if an excellent level of service has been provided, although this is entirely discretionary. A 15% gratuity is charged automatically on all beverage tabs, including dining room wine accounts.

Cruising

Regent Seven Seas Cruises

🖱 www.rssc.com

RSSC includes all shipboard gratuities in the cost of its cruises so there is no tipping on board the company's ships unless a guest feels that exceptional service has been given. The company stresses that there is no obligation to offer a gratuity, but advises that if guests feel uncomfortable about not giving gratuities they can contribute to the Crew Welfare Fund which exists aboard each vessel. The fund is used for crew parties.

Royal Caribbean International

🖱 www.royalcaribbean.com

Royal Caribbean has developed gratuity guidelines to make things easier for passengers on board its ships. They can be paid in three ways: prepaid by having them added to the reservation made by the passenger's booking agent; added to the onboard SeaPass account at any time during the cruise; or paid in cash at the end of the cruise. The company suggests that suitable tips per person per day for key members of staff might be as follows: US$5.75 for a suite attendant, US$3.50 for the stateroom attendant and dining room waiter, US$2 for the assistant waiter, and US$0.75 for the head waiter. Additionally, a service charge of 15% is applied to all bar and wine bills. Gratuities to all other staff such as the spa and casino teams are left to guests' discretion.

Cruising

Saga Cruises

🖰 **www.saga.co.uk**

Around 80% of the passengers aboard the ships of this UK cruise line are from Britain, with the remainder mostly from North America. Programmes are tailored for an over-50s clientele. The company says that gratuities are included in the fare and additional tipping is not expected. If passengers wish to make gratuities it is entirely at their discretion.

Seabourn Cruise Line

🖰 **www.seabourn.com**

Seabourn Cruise Line, which has luxury ships sailing around the Mediterranean, Caribbean, northern Europe, the Americas and transatlantic routes, says gratuities are included in the package fares quoted. If passengers wish to make private gratuities then this is entirely discretionary, but the culture on board is that no further tips are expected. Indeed, staff are encouraged to politely decline, so do not be offended if they do.

Silversea Cruises

🖰 **www.silversea.com**

Silversea Cruises includes all amounts for gratuities to staff in the cost of the cruise, and guests should feel under no obligation to tip further. In fact, offering gratuities on board the company's luxury cruiseships is frowned upon.

Cruising

Spirit of Adventure and Quest of Adventure

🖱 www.spiritofadventure.com

This company, which offers adventure cruises throughout the Mediterranean, the Caribbean, the Americas and even Antarctica, has a no-tipping policy on board its ships, so guests are under no obligation to offer gratuities.

Star Clippers

🖱 www.starclippers.co.uk

This sailing ship line recommends €8 per person per night (around US$10.50), which is divided between the cabin steward and the waiter. Passengers can tip either by cash at the end of the cruise or by having the specified amount charged to their shipboard account. The company specialises in, as its name suggests, cruises on board beautiful clipper sailing tall ships.

Swan Hellenic

🖱 www.swanhellenic.com

With an ever-changing fleet of small ships, this company has been sailing the waters of the world for over 50 years. It offers no guidelines for expressing thanks to staff members who have shown exceptional service, but says it is happy should guests feel they would like to tip staff. The practice and the amount is entirely at the guests' discretion.

Cruising

Thomson

🖰 **www.thomson.co.uk**

The cruising division of this mainstream holiday package company offers cruises throughout the world. Gratuities are included in all the quoted prices and distributed fairly amongst staff, but the company suggests that if exceptional service has been provided by any member of staff during a cruise and passengers wish to reward this with a discretionary sum of money, then this is entirely acceptable.

Viking River Cruises

🖰 **www.vikingrivercruises.co.uk**

This company has been offering river cruises around the world, including in countries such as Russia, Ukraine and China, for more than a decade. It doesn't offer any guidelines for passengers' gratuities, preferring to leave guests the option of tipping key members of staff at their discretion. Such tips would be in cash and given at the end of the cruise.

Windstar Cruises

🖰 **www.windstarcruises.com**

Windstar Cruises feels gratuities should be left to passengers' discretion and offers no guidelines as such, but recommends that tips should be along the lines followed by other luxury cruise lines. The company says it prefers that guests should be free to reward exceptional service. It does, however, take a hard line if any member of staff is found to be soliciting tips.

Cruising

Just some of our destinations

Index

Countries

A
Albania 48
Algeria 2
Angola 3
Argentina 166
Armenia 132
Australia 133
Austria 49
Azores 51

B
Bahamas 184
Bahrain 116
Bangladesh 134
Belarus 52
Belgium 54
Belize 167
Benin 4
Bermuda 185
Bolivia 168
Borneo 135
Bosnia &
  Herzegovina 56
Botswana 5
Brazil 169
Bulgaria 57

C
Cameroon 7
Canada 186
Cape Verde 8
Carriacou 193
Cayman Islands 187
Chile 170
China 136
Colombia 171
Costa Rica 172
Croatia 58
cruising 203–18
  see also individual

company listings,
  below
Cuba 188
Cyprus 60
Czech Republic 62

D
Denmark 64
Dominica 190
Dominican Republic
  191

E
Ecuador 173
Egypt 9
Eritrea 12
Estonia 65
Ethiopia 13

F
Faroe Islands 66
Finland 67
France 68

G
Gambia, the 14
Georgia 138
Germany 71
Ghana 15
Gozo 88
Greece 73
Grenada 193
Guyana 174

H
Hong Kong 136
Hungary 75

I
Iceland 78
India 139
Indonesia 140
Iran 117
Ireland, Republic of
  79

Israel 118
Italy 81

J
Jamaica 194
Japan 141
Jordan 119

K
Kazakhstan 143
Kenya 16
Kyrgyzstan 144

L
Latvia 83
Lebanon 121
Liberia 18
Libya 19
Lithuania 84
Luxembourg 86

M
Macedonia 87
Madagascar 20
Malawi 22
Malaysia 145
Maldives 146
Mali 23
Malta 88
Mauritius 24
Mexico 196
Mongolia 148
Montenegro 90
Morocco 25
Mozambique 27

N
Namibia 28
Nepal 149
Netherlands, the 91
New Zealand 151
Nigeria 29
Norway 93